The Aesthetic Blueprint

The Game-changing Guide to Transforming Your Practice, Living a Fulfilling Life and Impacting the Lives of Everyone You Touch

By Robert R. Rullo

Ordering Information & Quantity Sales: Special discounts are available on quantity purchases by corporations, associations, and others. For details, contact the publisher. Orders by U.S. & International trade bookstores and wholesalers at: info@abundantpress.com. Printed in the United States of America- Library of Congress-in-Publication Data

Title: The Aesthetic Blueprint
Subtitle: *The Game-changing Guide to Transforming Your Practice, Living a Fulfilling Life and Impacting the Lives of Everyone You Touch.*
Author: Robert R. Rullo
1. The main category of the book — Business, Medical
First Printing 9-25-2018 - Second Printing 10-20-2018
ISBN: 978-1-948287-07-4

Disclaimer

Although the author(s) and publisher have made every effort to ensure that the information in this book was correct at press time. While we try to keep the information up-to-date and correct, there are no representations or warranties, express or implied, about the completeness, accuracy, reliability, suitability or availability with respect to the information. The author and publisher are NOT providing tax, legal, financial or investment advice, do not assume and hereby disclaim any liability to any party for any loss, damage, or disruption caused by errors or omissions, whether such errors or omissions result from negligence, accident, or any other cause. Nothing else contained in this book should be used or construed as an offer to sell, a solicitation of an offer to buy, or a recommendation for any security. Nor is it intended as investment, tax, financial or legal advice. Investors should seek such professional advice for their particular situation.

This book is for informational purposes only. This book should not be considered a solicitation, offer or recommendation for the purchase or sale of any securities or other financial products and services discussed herein. Readers of this book will not be considered clients of Robert R. Rullo and/or Rullo Communications or continuED Medical LLC. just by virtue of access to this book. Information contained herein is not intended for persons in any jurisdiction where such distribution or use would be contrary to the laws or regulations of that jurisdiction. Readers should not construe any discussion or information contained herein as personalized advice Robert R. Rullo and/or Rullo Communications or continuED Medical LLC. Neither our information providers nor we shall be liable for any errors or inaccuracies, regardless of cause, or the lack of timeliness of, or for any delay or loss of income.

Certain information contained in this book is derived from sources that Robert R. Rullo and/or Rullo Communications or continuED Medical LLC. believes to be reliable; however, Robert E. Rullo and/or Rullo Communications or continuED Medical LLC. does not guarantee the accuracy or timeliness of such information and assumes no liability for any resulting damages. Readers should seek advice regarding the appropriateness of investing in any securities or other financial instruments referred to in this book, website or any other message received from Robert R. Rullo and/or Rullo Communications or continuED Medical LLC.and should understand that statements regarding future prospects of these or other financial products may not be realized. Legal Disclosure you are hereby advised that Robert R. Rullo and/or Rullo Communications or continuED Medical LLC. is not a financial advisor and is NOT providing legal or tax advice. Nothing in this book or its attachments should be interpreted by you as legal advice. For legal advice and all legal related matters, Robert R. Rullo and/or Rullo Communications or continuED Medical LLC. Recommends that you seek the advice of a qualified attorney licensed in your state or jurisdiction.

For additional information & bonus content please visit:

AestheticBlueprintBook.com

TABLE OF CONTENTS

DEDICATION

To Rich Rullo (1928 – 2008)

"And he gave to me a gift I know I never can repay."

Dan Fogelberg,

Lyric from Leader of the Band

ACKNOWLEDGEMENTS

I am extremely grateful to all of those who inspired me to write this, my first book.

So many offered to help and support me as I learned the process of authorship. Their friendship and grace far and away exceeded anything I could have expected.

To my family, who stand by me regardless. To my wife Anne, daughters Stephanie, Joanna and her husband Chris, and Anneli. To my son Richard and his wife Mary Catherine. And my handsome grandson, Charlie. My mom, Esther and siblings Dan, Janette, and Jimmy and their families. God bless you all!

To my dear, dear friend, Toni Nouri who has been by my side (and I, hers) for more years than I can remember. Your supreme professsionalism is only surpassed by your warm friendly nature and undying friendship. Thank you Toni for your gifts of patience and support and your role as chief editor of this book.

Randy Woo, our weekly calls kept me focused on the prize and I'm grateful for your guidance and "coaching me up" – when I needed it most.

Thanks to Jessica Haapanen who first presented me with the idea of writing a book. Your thoughts and 'push' were the initial inspiration behind this work and for that I'm grateful. To Sarah Caples who provided me with some tools for book writing that were extremely helpful when I began this process.

Melanie Hall, although we never met in person, I thank you for your wonderful content editing and feedback on the first draft and those thereafter. So grateful that I found you.

To Jay Abraham, *Success* magazine was spot on in calling you *"the greatest marketing mind alive today"*. Your counsel, remarkable insight and friendship have taken The Aesthetic Blueprint to a whole new level of being outstanding.

Thank you to Andrew Davis, a best selling author who graciously agreed to write the Forward to this book. Andrew, you are an absolute brilliant mind with a beautiful soul who has taught me a ton in his own unique way.

To Alonzo Cahoon for helping me understand the importance and value of setting and keeping a high standard everyday. Presence and persistence. Who do I get to be today?

To Kent Remington, MD, Arthur Swift, MD and Stephen Marquardt, MD. You taught me to look beyond the obvious through the lessons of the great ones like Di Vinci and Michaelanglo.

Deberah Bringelson for your encouragement and helping me see the gift of positive energy and attraction. So grateful to you.

To Danine Summers and Diane Foster whose support and encouragement got this whole train a-runnin'.

To the many authors, keynote speakers and visonaries whom I admire and respect. At the top of that list are Tony and Sage Robbins, who have touched my life and millions of others in a very profound way. Simon Sinek, I've been inspired by Why and will spend the rest of my days helping others find theirs. Jack Canfield, David Meerman Scott, Jeff Kaufman, Robert Cialdini, Steve Sims, Denise Lee Yohn, Tim Ferris, Stephen Covey, Dan Pink, Coach John Wooden, Peter Diamandis, Dr. Joe Vitale, Donald Miller, Dr. Joe Dispenza, Dr. Freddy Behin, Marissa Levin and Gino Wickman all have provided perspective that inspired the contents of this book. Thank you all.

To Padre Pio. You were my Dad's favorite saint and mine too.

And finally, to my best friend, Karen Bickford. I saved you for last. Since the day we met you've been both my biggest fan and my biggest critic. I never know which one will show up but I know most importantly that you will -- everytime. Words can't express my gratitude for your unbridled determination to make me great.

God Bless You All.

FORWARD

If there's one thing I've learned in the last twenty years as a marketer, it's that there are no silver bullets. There are no shortcuts, quick tips, hacks or simple solutions that truly transform a business.

So what is it that molds ordinary businesses into overnight successes?

They all understand an honest marketing truth: you don't have to offer the best products or procedures, you don't even have to have the latest technology or the fanciest address, but you do have to deliver the best experience.

That's right. The boldest, most successful businesses in the world sell experiences, not products or services.

The fact is, most aesthetic practitioners are good at telling people why their practice is different. The problem is, they're no good at showing people how it's different. Because at the end of the day you sell a commodity.

In fact, you don't sell microdermabrasion or Botox. You don't sell face-lifts or tummy tucks. You don't even sell tattoo or laser hair removal. You sell an experience.

Great experiences are self-selecting, they're higher-value.
Referrable experiences are clearly communicated and more easily ownable. But most importantly, a fantastic experience lasts longer and means more to you, your clients, and your future.

The Aesthetic Blueprint isn't a shortcut or a hack. It doesn't contain a checklist of easy-to-complete items that will take your practice from profitable to prolific. It's an honest, open, and transparent path to uncovering what makes you and your practice unique.

What Bob has done in this book isn't easy and what he prescribes isn't simple. He asks questions that will make you uncomfortable. He assigns exercises that force you to reflect and re-think. The Aesthetic Blueprint is designed to challenge you. Are you up for the challenge?

Because if you are, the outcome won't just be a more successful practice, you'll build a better experience. An experience that inspires, joy, interest, and approval from everyone you touch.

Andrew Davis
Bestselling author of Brandscaping: Unleashing the Power of Partnerships and TOWN INC.

INTRODUCTION

"Don't wait for extraordinary opportunities.
Seize common occasions and make them great."
— Orison Swett Marden, American Author

One morning, Mary, a 47-year-old middle manager, stares longingly into her bathroom mirror. "Mirror, mirror on the wall" she mutters to herself, quoting the Evil Queen from Snow White. As she peers into the mirror, she is saddened by what she sees. She knows that she didn't win the DNA lottery but c'mon. This? At age 47, still young at heart, she examines each and every wrinkle. She sees every one of them. *Even the ones that aren't really there.* She steps back a bit to notice how the shape of her face has actually changed. "Mary, what's happened to you?" she says softly to the mirror. Now her mind wanders away from the mirror, as if almost in a deep trance and she thinks about her life, her career, her successes, her failures, her joy, her disappointments, her family, and her friends.

She sighs recalling how she was bypassed for a job promotion, despite the fact that she believed that she was more qualified.

Then, just for a moment, she goes back in time, thinking of her high school days and all the joys and drama that came with it and how long ago that seemed. She smiles a bit breaking her trance only to find herself still staring at this aging face in her bathroom mirror. Her smile quickly leaves, replaced by a furrowed brow.

At that very moment, Mary makes a decision. She is no longer going to be "plain 'ole middle management" Mary – just aging away. Not anymore. She has decided to change fate, her look, and her outlook to feel more youthful. She is going to seek cosmetic treatment.

Like most patients, Mary has trepidation about her decision. She is unfamiliar with most cosmetic procedures, and from what she seen on television or on the internet, a good deal of it seems deceptive or sensationalized. Mary is skeptical of "Before/After" photos, fearing misrepresentation of the truth. In malls and other public venues, she sees frighteningly poor results that give her pause and almost force her to reconsider this crazy notion. "After all, who am I to think I can look better?" she asks herself. However, this time she is determined.

She does her research – committed to finding the right practice, the right practitioner who will fulfill her dream of looking and most importantly, feeling better about herself. She "googles" and reads. She "yelps" and reads.

She views specific patient-focused sites like RealSelf, watches videos on YouTube, and chats with others online with similar interests via social networks. She hesitantly speaks with close friends and others who might have recommendations based on their collective experience and more. Finally, after an exhaustive exercise to find the right practice, she selects the one that she believes best meets her needs and can solve her problem. She is confident that this is the practice best suited for her. But with that confidence comes more trepidation fraught with a litany of questions like, "is this going to hurt?," "how much is this going to cost?," "am I really going to look better?," "what do I do if I'm not happy?," "yikes, is this really the right thing to do?"

However, committed to her outcome, she picks up the phone, calls the number and makes an appointment to be seen. It's now the day of the appointment. She's thought long and hard about her decision and despite frequent thoughts of reconsideration, she's goes to the appointment. Her confidence in her decision has grown since her initial phone conversation with a practice receptionist who was friendly and quite knowledgeable.

In fact, she felt like she knew her already as a friend. Her confidence in her decision grew even more when she entered the meticulously kept and well-designed office, which looked, smelled, sounded and felt like a resort spa rather than a medical office. She reconnected with the receptionist who greeted her with a warm smile.

They share a story. She thinks to herself, "Yeah, I could go out for drinks with her." She's shocked to find that she doesn't have to sit and wait. Hold on, you always have to wait in a doctor's office, right? She smiles even brighter as she is escorted by the practice concierge to meet her doctor. Like the receptionist, the practice concierge is warm and friendly, offering to answer any questions she might have. They chat a bit. "I could have drinks with her too!" she says smiling to herself.

So far, she is happy with her decision. The experience so far has been great. However, what she doesn't realize is that the best is yet to come, and it begins with a soft knock on the door . . .

Fast-forward 11 years later. It's a new Mary. She feels confident, assured and comfortable in her own skin. Her taste in fashion has changed for the better. She is flattered by questions from admirers like "what's your secret?" or "did you just get back from vacation?" or "you never seem to change." Most importantly, her inner beauty has been unleashed, shining brightly through her every day. Her family and friends enjoy the warm, connected and engaging new Mary.

During this 11-year journey, Mary remained committed to her outcome. Her treatment plan was progressive, with each treatment slowly but surely enhancing the one before. She is well entrenched in the maintenance phase of her treatment and has been for a while, now simply looking fantastic for her age.

Mary is grateful for the amazing turnaround that she has created.
This morning, Mary gazes into her bathroom mirror – "Mirror, mirror on the wall" she laughs out loud.

Postscript

The story above is representative of the aspirations, desires, motivations, and concerns of the many souls seeking cosmetic treatment. Their decisions are often fraught with doubt and a variety of other kinds of concerns. Despite this uncertainty, they are driven by a want or a need or a desire to find a solution to a problem – their problem – the one that keeps them awake at night. In some cases, the problem is merely a cosmetic one – someone seeking to look better.

In other cases, the problem is much, much deeper – rebounding from divorce, a breakup, layoffs, or promotion bypass. All of these have a profound visceral impact along with a strong desire to find a solution, feel better, look better, and become more alive!

As aesthetic practitioners, you have the ability to create all of this. How amazing is it that you can literally improve someone's life – not just their health, but the way they view the world and live their lives, impacting the lives around them?

However, here's the other side of this true story. During that 11-year engagement with her cosmetic practitioner, Mary, an average wage earner, middle manager, spent over $100,000 in treatments. That's right, more than $100,000.

Here's an important point. There are $100,000 patients out there looking for you, right now! They are determined to get the best cosmetic result possible and are searching desperately to find the right practice to change their life. Yes, they are out there, and they are searching for you as you read this text.

How can you create a $100,000 patient? Better yet, how can you create one hundred $100,000 patients or better yet, 1,000 of these patients?

The answer lies within these pages.

However, first you have to . . . wake up!

Stop just for a second and ask yourself this simple question: is my practice truly where I want it to be? Am I at full throttle but not seeing the results I want? If so, what's the problem?

Alternatively, perhaps you are the best in town or the best in the state or the best in the country. Congratulations, you are breathing rarified air! So my question to you then is, "So what's next?" Is there another level for you? The answer is yes, there is.

However, here's the problem.
The aesthetic marketplace is in a flat spin. Better yet, a rapid downward spiral.

Wait a second? How is it possible for an industry so young and bountiful to be sinking so fast?

How is it possible that an industry with a new major advancement launched seemingly every week, is headed rapidly for commoditization?

That defies all business logic, but make no mistake: the practice of aesthetic medicine is quickly becoming commoditized. Yes, commoditized like soap powder, razor blades laundry detergent and diapers.

Commoditization: \kə-ˌmä-də-tə-ˈzā-shən\ -- Almost total lack of meaningful differentiation in the manufactured goods. Commoditized products have thin margins and are sold on the basis of price and not brand. This situation is characterized by standardized, ever cheaper, and common technology that invites more suppliers who lower the prices even further.

So what's the deal? All data points suggest a considerable influx of patients interested in seeking cosmetic treatment – many interested in the nonsurgical offering. In 2016, Americans alone spent more than $15 billion on combined surgical and nonsurgical procedures for the first time, according to the American Society of Plastic Surgeons [ASPS] statistical database. (ASPS 2016) Nonsurgical procedures showed an overall increase of 7%, while injectables as a group were up 10%. These numbers are impressive and are consistent with the explosion of opportunity offered by the aesthetic marketplace.

Simply put, the aesthetic market is loaded with opportunity (and growing)! Why then are aesthetic practices all over North America struggling? Struggling to get new patients? Struggling to retain current clients? Struggling to find talented staff? Struggling, in some cases, to stay in business? The opportunities are abundant. The tools are readily available. In fact, technology has become so advanced that one can create results with a syringe that previously could only be accomplished through sophisticated surgery. New lasers and energy devices are readily available to treat almost any aesthetic abnormality.

On the surface, the business of aesthetics appears to be the quintessential paradox. Actually, the situation is pretty straightforward, and surprisingly, so is the solution. This book has been written to provide you the reader with a blueprint for improving the way you practice aesthetics. More specifically, the way you practice the *business* of aesthetics. This is not a teaching manual on practice management, or a recipe for success or some other off-the-shelf business color-by-numbers text. Rather, it contains proven strategies to growing one's business – any business.

The concepts herein have made companies like Apple, Zappos, and Starbucks the respected market leaders that they are.

What's do all of these successful brands have in common? What's the key to their universal success?

Differentiation. The key is differentiation. That's right. The antidote to commoditization is differentation. Being different from the rest. Do things in a different way then the rest of the market. Breaking the rules, raising the bar, ignoring what many call 'common sense' and ultimately creating a new standard for the market. These are game changers and game chargers are without a doubt, daring to be different.
Not for the sake of differentiation but for the sake of adding greater value to their clients than anyone else.

I specifically chose to use the word 'blueprint' because it best describes the goal of this book. That objective is to offer you battle-tested strategies that, if followed with discipline (more on this later), will enable you to create major breakthroughs and find significant growth opportunities for your practice. Ultimately, you will be one of the few swimming against the tide of aesthetic commoditization (and reaping the financial rewards).

First a little background: I have spent the last three decades learning the business of business. During this time, I have had the privilege to work with some of the top companies in the healthcare industry and study with bona fide thought leaders from a variety of medical specialties. However, of all these renowned experts, none have impressed me with their clinical expertise and business acumen more than B. Kent Remington, MD and Arthur Swift, MD. So much so, that with their guidance, I built the preeminent training course in aesthetics today aptly named **The Aesthetic Blueprint™**.

Here's our story.

For years I believed that medicine fell short in creating a great experience for patients. I believed that patients did better and healed faster if in fact, they had a great experience and trusting relationship with their healthcare provider – meaning that the practitioner provided more than just treatment.

I became fasinated with aesthetics for it truly was the only medical specialty that literally could 'heal a patient's soul'.

Then in 2009, shortly after I started my new medical education company continuED Medical LLC, a professional associate of mine, Danine Summers, then head of medical affairs at Medicis, suggested that I contact a cosmetic dermatologist in Calgary, Alberta. My initial thought was "what value could there possibly be in speaking with a Canadian dermatologist?" With some reluctance, I dialed the number – not ever knowing that the voice on the other end would be a voice that would send me on a fascinating journey that I am still on today. That voice was none other than Dr. B. Kent Remington. I knew within a few minutes that I was speaking to a sage. Not just a "thought leader" . . . but a sage. The thoughts and insights he readily shared with me introduced me to a whole new dimension of aesthetics and understanding of the business of aesthetics. Over an hour later, our scheduled 10-minute introductory call ended with him telling me something that I will never forget.

"In aesthetics, if you focus on making money, you'll never create a great result, but if you focus on creating a great result, you'll make a lot of money."

That closed the deal for me, and as I hung up the phone, I knew that I wanted to partner with this man. To be honest, since then, he has given me so many great quotes about the business of aesthetics and life in general (which I will share throughout this book), but none had more impact on me than focusing on creating a great result. In fact, that statement alone ultimately has become the motto (or fight song) of the training we have developed called The Aesthetic Blueprint.

Shortly after that, Kent introduced me to my other professional soulmate Arthur Swift, MD – another Canadian. Arthur, a plastic surgeon by training, has an amazing practice in Montreal and is invited to speak and teach all over the world. From Arthur, I learned the concept of BeautiPHIcation™ and the mathematics of beauty, in that there is an approach that can be followed to measure beauty, and in the aging face, the loss of volume and other facial changes that ultimately reflect in a loss of beauty. (Swift & Remington, 2011)

He introduced me to the concept of Phi and how Phi proportions can be measured using calipers – the same calipers used by the artists and sculptors of the Renaissance era. He artfully described the Golden Ratio and how it is reflected in art and design and importantly, how it consistently crosses all genres in defining beauty.

The concept of Phi to my knowledge had rarely been taught in aesthetics and fueled my growing belief that aesthetics, more so than any other medical specialty, was more than the true merger of art and science – it was the true merger of art, science, and design.

For it is the design of your practice – why and how you practice – that truly makes the difference in today's competitive aesthetic marketplace.

The more I worked with Kent and Arthur, the more I realized that their teachings were more than just theory or belief. The lessons they shared were tested through trial and error, learning from mistakes and most importantly challenging the norm. It is this latter concept, challenging the norm that became the foundation of The Aesthetic Blueprint and, frankly, this book.

As we worked together, a second epiphany occured to me: that wanting to be truly successful in aesthetics – to truly be an elite practice – one needed to be not only a great clinician/technician but a great businessperson as well. Not just the mechanics of business but the spirit of business. After all, business is a spiritual venture. Read that line again.

Successful brands, those that have successfully sustained themselves for the long haul, have been built on the spirit of the company, its people and the people that they serve.

The very best aesthetic practices not only understand this concept, but also embrace it and live it. Unfortunately, many aesthetic practices, especially the mediocre ones that struggle, do not get this concept, viewing it as a soft or squishy idea, irrelevant to the success of their business. This is truly unfortunate in that it may be the most essential component of owning and running an extremely successful and profitable aesthetic practice.

After working with numerous practices and clients desiring to grow their business and in many cases taking their practice to the next level, I understood that an initiative focusing on the business of aesthetics would be beneficial. This type of training would go beyond traditional accounting and tactical market planning. Instead its design would focus on creating an extraordinary experience for the ultimate client, the patient.

The idea that people don't buy products or services, rather they buy an identity and an experience, is the cornerstone of this book (more on this later).

The book is designed to focus on this very simple concept. Once you understand, embrace and live this idea of creating a great experience in today's marketplace, all of the other business-related issues fall into place.

The book is written with this spirit in mind and is built on the concept of core values that support a vision you will create for your practice. Regardless of your location, the size of your practice or the number of years you have been in practice, the concepts and ideas herein are useful to you.

These are customizable and manageable to fit your specific needs. However, make no mistake that the bedrock of this information remains solely focused on the importance creating a great experience for your patients, much in the way that Apple, the Four Seasons Hotel, The Ritz-Carlton, and other high-end consumer-focused brands have been successful. Your practice can use the same ideas and concepts regardless of its size. Incorporate them successfully to not only get new patients or clients, but create a sense of loyalty among your current clients who will want to spend more with you and importantly refer their friends and acquaintances.

As part of The Aesthetic Blueprint training course, I have spent hours studying the concept of creating a great experience as a differentiator and the antidote to the commoditization of aesthetics. Moreover, although our immersion seminars are wildly successful, by design we still only reach a small, targeted audience of advanced practitioners.

This book is written to share those experiences with a broader audience enabling them to understand these business concepts, which if incorporated with a Spartan-like discipline can change the way you practice aesthetics for the good.

It is my hope that you find the information herein not only usable from a strategic perspective, but also as an inspiration to expand your practice to the next level.

It is important to say here that regardless of past successes or the number of years you have been in practice, there is indeed another level of success awaiting you. Importantly, there is a blueprint to follow to get you there. But really, talk is cheap! Where the results are seen are in those practices that embrace these concepts, live these concepts and share them as part of their day-to-day activities and interactions with their patients.

The essence of this book is that success in any business including aesthetics focuses primarily on the mindset of the business owner. If you are a dabbler in business, meaning that you try something here and then try something there, this book will be of no value to you.

However, if you are willing to embrace these concepts full heartedly, teach them to your staff and demand their commitment, you will be amazed at how quickly you can grow your business. Ultimately the decision of how successful your practice can be rests on your shoulders.

This cannot be delegated to a practice manager or another high-level employee in your practice; it must come from you regardless of your leadership skills.

The tools and strategies offered in this book are proven and will work for anyone who follows that with a commitment and desire for creating success.

I hope that you, dear reader, will quickly see the opportunity before you and utilize this information and leverage the expertise from which it was drawn to grow your practice exponentially.

As a personal and business coach to aesthetic practices, I have encountered numerous issues or what I call blind spots that confront my clients. Interestingly there are some of these blind spots that occur with high frequency.

The Common Blindspots Choking Your Practice

1) Failure to wholly understand your patients/clients wants or needs;

2) Not creating the ultimate experience for your patients/clients;

3) Forgetting that you are the most important salesperson in the practice;

4) A Weak Fragmented Culture; and

5) The Success Log Jam is You

Given their high frequency and commonality, these blind spots form the chapters of this book and are shared so that you too can address them with vigor.

Chapter 1: *Truly Understanding Your Patients'/Clients' Wants and Needs*

Chapter 2: *Creating The Ultimate Customer Experience*

Chapter 3: *You Are The Most Important Sales Person in Your Practice*

Chapter 4: *Culture is King*; and

Chapter 5: *It Begins With You*

You will be surprised to see that most of these challenges are internal and self-induced, which is good news because you can control and significantly impact the outcome in a positive way.

Obviously there are external factors that you cannot control, but if you address them as opportunities – not problems, your practice will explode with exponential growth. So while everyone else is running for the hills, you are basking in the light of success.

One final thought. If you read this book 20 years from now – the principles and teachings wherein will still apply. That's how essential this book is to creating significant growth in your practice – in any economy.

So . . . opportunity awaits you. Now the question becomes: what are you prepared to do?

-- Robert R. Rullo

For additional information & bonus content please visit:

AestheticBlueprintBook.com

CHAPTER 1:
Truly Understanding Your Patients'/Clients' Wants and Needs

"Don't find customers for your products,
find products for your customers."
— Seth Godin

On a cold winter morning in January 2007, a young man began to play his violin in the hallway at the Metro in Washington, DC during rush hour. He played for nearly 45 minutes as almost 1,000 commuters hurried by without even noticing.

During that time, only six people stopped to listen for a while, and 27 gave money totaling a whopping $32. He played six pieces, several from Bach and each piece ended in silence -- no applause or outward signs of appreciation or recognition. Passers-by hurried to catch their trains to life's destination.

What those harried commuters failed to realize was that this young violinist was none other than internationally renowned virtuoso Joshua Bell, recognized today as one of the world's greatest musicians. As part of a study on social behavior, Bell, disguised wearing a baseball cap, agreed to appear at the train station incognito to play some of the most intricate pieces of music ever written with his handcrafted 1713 Stradivarius violin worth $3.5 million!

A few days earlier, Bell performed to a packed house at Boston Symphony Hall – ticket prices topping at well over $100 and a waitlist.

However, at the DC Metro, hardly anyone noticed. Acoustics aside, wasn't it the same beautiful music played at the Boston Symphony Hall a few days earlier?

Approximately seven years later, Bell returned to Washington DC, this time as himself to perform an advertised 30-minute free concert at Union Station. Over 1000 people packed the train station's main hall to see Bell joined by nine other string players for an outstanding musical experience.

"I wanted to show that even though the surroundings are similar, if you have active people who are really there to listen you have a wonderful experience, and it turned out much better than I could have imagined," Bell said later in an interview.

As business owners, what can be learned from the Joshua Bell experiment? Several things actually. First, people do judge a book by its cover. Once those commuters knew the performance was indeed the real Joshua Bell, they flocked to hear his music even though the venue was virtually the same. The fact that this was not an acoustically well-fitted concert hall did not matter. Despite the music being the same, those commuters had a greater appreciation because now they KNEW it was Bell, not some transient playing in the train station for money.

How often as aesthetic practitioners do we act like those commuters and miss wonderful opportunities that sit right before us. How often do we treat patients like patients and not like clients? This is not a matter of mere semantics. Rather, it is a mindset that if adopted, can change your practice for the better forever. As a practitioner, you were trained to treat patients; to astutely diagnose their illness and swiftly and appropriately treat it. Thus, success is measured by the elimination of the illness or specific issue causing the illness.

Depending on your beliefs, that measurement of success is commonplace throughout healthcare. However, with the advent of aesthetic medicine, the landscape of "treatment" has changed, and the usual rules of treatment only partly apply.

Granted, one can still follow traditional rules and be modestly successful, but if you genuinely want to make a difference then you have got to go beyond – I mean well beyond – what you were taught in medical school.

You must now think of your patients as clients. Not customers – but clients. Patients are people you treat. Customers are one-time buyers, but *clients are dedicated to you.* It is a big difference. Moreover, even within this client pool lies an even more significant group of people I call **Raving Fans**. Raving Fans are a super group of clients who trust you unconditionally, are completely loyal to you, will defend you, are willing to recommend you to their friends and importantly are the first to forgive you. These are your $100,000 patients. Create this Raving Fan base and watch your practice grow to levels that you could previously only dream of.

So how do you create Raving Fans?

Answer: You need to know them better than anyone. You need to understand their wants, needs, and problems completely, and then deliver beyond their expectations. I am not talking about good quality care or great customer service – EVERYONE claims that.

That is not different. I am talking about a deeper connection, a deeper understanding of their wants, needs, problems, and desires, so deep in fact, that it emits an emotion. Connect at that level and watch the entire game change. If you can connect with someone on a deep emotional level, really and truly understand his or her needs (and I mean real needs), and deliver beyond their expectations, then wow, you have won the game! You have created a Raving Fan.

However, here's the problem. Many don't have the first clue about how to connect on a deeply personal level.

An article a few years back revealed a huge disconnect between what practitioners thought patients wanted versus what patients actually wanted. The article published in *Aesthetic Surgery Journal* by Kurkjian et al. in 2011. (Kurkjian et al. 2011) compared results from surveys given to both patients and practitioners. The findings are frankly stunning. The authors reported, "Surprisingly, the surveys [also] revealed that physician knowledge of patient preferences differs widely from actual patient preferences in terms of treatment costs and longevity." The authors went on to say that "it's worth noting that many patients would accept higher costs if it was correlated with longer lasting results."

I was struck by these findings as I hear all too often the self-limiting story that "patients won't pay for treatments" or the economy is blamed for lack of substantial practice growth. Know this, the growth of your practice is directly correlated to how well you as the business owner have connected with your clients – how well you and your team have created a Raving Fan base with your "patients." In my experience, this is single-handedly the main reason why practices fail to thrive – not really knowing and understanding the client.

You can attend all the clinical conferences you want. You can get all the hands-on expert injection training available and buy the latest, hottest new laser or energy device, but if you fail to connect with your clients on a deep emotional level – welcome to the world of mediocrity.

So what is the blueprint for creating a Raving Fan base? How do you connect with "patients" on a deep emotional level?

Spend time.

I am amazed at how little time most aesthetic practitioners spend with their patients. Aesthetic medicine is not a sprint; it is a well-run marathon.

After giving a talk on Creating Raving Fans during one of our Immersion Seminars in Scottsdale, I was approached by an attendee who shared that she, as the doctor and business owner, does not do patient consults, instead she relegates this responsibility to her nurses and medical assistants. HUGE MISTAKE. If you delegate this vital role to your staff, you will never, ever create Raving Fans.

I don't care what kind of clinical results you create; you'll never create Raving Fans. Why? Because in today's consumer market, people want more than just your product or service – they want an emotional connection with you – the practice owner, with you the practitioners, with you the brand.

Don't get me wrong; well-trained staff could play a vital role in the consult and the initial building of trust with the patient/client. However, YOU must make the ultimate connection.

To be fair, this is NOT your fault. You were trained in medical school to diagnose, treat, cure and move on. For example, most dermatologists that I work with can spot a skin condition from across the room. They could be writing the prescription or treatment plan as they walk across the room to greet the patient and be done with the examination. Done! However, aesthetics doesn't work that way because to be "crazy successful" requires a connection. Deep connection. Moreover, the only way to get that level of connection is to spend time with each patient during that initial consult and during every consult and interaction thereafter.

I recently spoke at Phil Wershler's A+MD conference in Coeur d'Alene, Idaho and had the opportunity to listen to a panel discussion with several experts in aesthetics. One of the questions asked was, "how long does your initial consult last?" I was surprised to see several of the responders trying to quantify their response, in other words, trying to give an actual timeframe or time limit.

Again, WRONG. One panel member finally gave the right answer, and that was, "as long as necessary." Although not perfect, that response to me warranted a standing ovation (though I just stayed in my seat and mentally applauded!). As flippant as that response might appear, it was exactly correct.

By now you are saying to yourself, then all I would do is spend time in consults and not treating patients (or making money). OK, you are right but here's the trick. If you prepare the patient in advance, have your staff conduct a preliminary consult (see, there is great value to using your staff after all), and ask thoughtful questions of the patient, then his/her responses will be an immediate identifier as to how much time you need to allow for that patient.

As Dr. Remington says, some patients are wired for aesthetics – meaning they are definitely looking to you, thus, making that emotional connection and discovering the real reason for seeking your services rather quickly. Other patients/clients will require more time and effort. To me again, these are the people with whom if you connect with them and tap into their emotion will become fans for life. Finally, there are those patients/clients that you do not want as clients.

Literally, you should refer them elsewhere, preferably to the competition down the street. These patients will reveal themselves early in the discussion if indeed you are asking the right questions and listening carefully. Here's the hard part – allowing yourself to decide to let that patient (and his/her business) walk out the door.

There's an adage in marketing that says, "Sometimes you have to fire your client." Intuitively this makes no sense in the competitive world of aesthetics but trust me by letting them walk you just saved yourself hundreds if not thousands of dollars, not to speak of the hours, sleepless nights, heartache and loss of staff respect.

Some patients just aren't the right fit and in the not-so-long-term become a drain on your time and resources with little gratitude and thanks in return. Deal with these patients with the same professional courtesy and thoughtfulness as you would any other patient and simply let them know that you are not able to help them and suggest (if appropriate) other options. It takes courage to allow patients to walk away, but you will be ahead – well ahead – in the long run.

Figuring out how much time to allow for a patient consult does take a little experience and a visceral feel but after a while, you will refine this skill and develop a blueprint for your consultations.

Can you have some success without profoundly connecting with patients? Probably yes. However, you just won't have Raving Fans; meaning that you will have to work harder to get more (new) patients and importantly retain the ones you have (and you will make less money).

Statistics show that it is much more cost effective to build a business based on repeat business versus finding brand new customers. In his book, Marketing Metrics, Paul Farris found that a **loyal customer has around a 60-70% conversion rate** – this is a staggering statistic in today's uncertain market place. Adobe did a similar study and found that loyal customers who have purchased from you twice before are **9 times more likely to convert** than first time customers. Clearly, developing loyalty from current clients pays big dividends regardless of the business you are in.

Become a Practical Psychologist.

To conduct a productive consult, one that inspires a patient/client to request and pay handsomely for your services, you have to become a practical psychologist. This means creating a deep connection with the patient/client. You've got to find out the real reason why the patient came to see you. Once you are able to uncover that real reason, a flood of emotion from that patient will flow.

Once they have shared that emotion (usually tears) with you, you have completed the first major step in building and gaining their absolute trust. As with any relationship, once an emotionally driven connection is made, a whole new bond is formed.

A few years back I learned a time- tested approach to understanding human behavior that applies perfectly to conducting an amazing patient consult, one that will create a Raving Fan.

This idea is built on the principle that business is really just about solving people's problems. Uber and Lyft started because of a problem. People hated the service or lack of service and hassle from traditional taxi companies. I bet you can think of more than one lousy experience with a taxi, right? Airbnb arose from the problem that hotel space during conventions in major cities was either incredibly expensive or virtually unavailable. So business grows out of the need to solve problems. However, it is more than that: these companies actually disrupt the market. They change the way business is done. What can you do to change the way the business of aesthetics is done? Here is a clue, you will never find the answer at a medical conference.

However, that is only half of the equation. To compete successfully you must truly understand your customer's problems and, importantly, have a deep understanding of their wants and needs – again, a deep understanding of their needs. Herein lies the challenge and the opportunity for creating a Raving Fan.

The approach is called Human Needs Psychology. I learned about Human Needs Psychology from Tony Robbins who refined it from years of studying human behavior and testing it in real time throughout the world during his fascinating seminars. (Robbins 2009). I give him credit for teaching it to me, and I am honored to share it with you. Human Needs Psychology is easy to understand and frankly easy to implement as part of your interactions with clients and your team. If you incorporate this approach into your consults and for that matter interaction with your staff and others, it will change the game for you.

Human Needs Psychology believes that fundamentally everyone on earth (regardless if you are the President of the United States or an aesthetic practitioner) has six human needs that drive their decisions and their daily actions. Meeting these needs is so powerful that some people will forego moral standards just to fulfill them, like for example cheating on a test.

Now, these needs are not merely wants or desires, they literally drive each and every decision and choice we make on a daily basis.

You are reading this book right now to fulfill one of the six human needs. Every decision, every action, every choice is rooted in the desire to satisfy these needs. You are where you are right now because of the decisions and choices you made to fulfill these six human needs. Remember, EVERYONE on planet Earth has these 6 human needs – Everyone.

By the way, it is important to know that although everyone has all of the six human needs, we don't value them all equally, which is the reason we all behave differently. However, many experts believe that most people have two dominant needs.

The six human needs are:

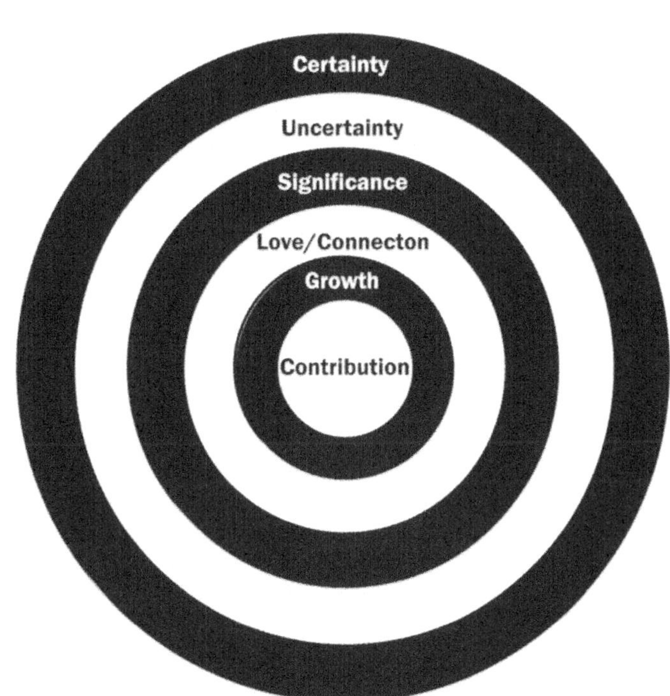

Certainty

Certainty is the need for safety, securing, stability, and consistency in one's life. If you are the type of person who looks for the exits after boarding an airplane, you have a high need for Certainty. If you have been employed by the same company for an extended time, you probably have a high need for Certainty.

Uncertainty

The next human need is Uncertainty: the need for variety, change, challenge, adventure, and surprise. Uncertainty sounds like a bit of a paradox to Certainty, and it is, yet humans have the need for both. Think of it this way: if you knew exactly what was going to happen virtually every moment of every day, day in and day out consistently, what would life be like? Right – more boring than you can imagine. I recall the 1993 hit movie *Groundhog Day* starring Bill Murray, who plays a boorish weather forecaster who relives Groundhog Day over and over again until he changes his unkind ways. Life for him became so predictable that he even attempted suicide because there was no longer any variety, thrill or uncertainty in his life. (By the way: 1. The movie is a comedy; and 2. I have been to Punxsutawney, Pennsylvania, where the real Groundhog Day is celebrated every February, and it is a great town!)

Significance

Significance is the need to feel special, unique, wanted, proud and recognized. I can tell you now that most of your aesthetic patients/clients probably value this need above all others, and it definitely is one of the driving forces to seek out your services. I believe that Significance is one of the six human needs that you can actually see visually. Note the tattoo and piercing cultures, sports cars, Versace purses, and $10,000 wristwatches – you don't have to look far to see Significance. Make a mental note of this statement, as we will revisit it again shortly.
As with the other human needs, people go about finding Significance in a variety of ways, some constructive, some neutral, and some destructive. For example, if someone points a gun at you, how significant are they? Others get Significance through service, giving of time or financial donations to a good cause.

I believe that, at least in our culture, achieving the need for Significance may be the primary and most sought after of the six Human Needs.

Love/Connection

Here is another paradox: since the need for Significance promotes individuality and being "different" from others to be special; it also drives the need for Love and Connection. Love and Connection is the need to be wanted, loved, connected and in some cases intimate with others. Some people struggle with fulfilling the needs of Significance and Love/Connection because they spend too much time seeking Significance and often risk the need for intimacy and deep connection. Do you wonder why divorce rates are high? Blame it on this Significane – Love/Connection human need paradox.

Growth

Simply put, if you are an inhabitant of Planet Earth, you are either growing or dying. Everything in nature is either growing or dying – there is no middle ground. Again, one of the reasons that you are taking time out of your life to read this book is to grow, to learn, to expand your horizons. If your practice/business isn't growing, it is dying. If you are not reevaluating, challenging, reassessing, redesigning, modifying, trying new things, you are dying. Resting on your laurels feels good for a moment, but without growth, your decline will soon begin.

At The Aesthetic Blueprint Immersion Seminars, I often speak of mastering the business skills of aesthetics. Too many practitioners want to dabble in their training. They come up with stories like loss of revenue for being away from the practice, or there's nothing new to learn, or lack of time. Training is the scaffolding to growth, to Mastery. Not just any training – training that genuinely challenges you, and with that challenge comes growth.

Importantly, your training is very important to your patients/clients! In fact, expertise and training consistently ranks highly among criterion that patients use when selecting a practitioner for aesthetic treatment.

Off the subject a bit, but have you ever used training you received as an advertising tool for your practice? If not, why not? You spent time, money and effort to attend. Hopefully, you learned something valuable. Why not tell your current and soon-to-be-new clients of that commitment and dedication you've made for them? Here's a clue – no one else is doing it either. Sound like an opportunity? Remember, if you are not growing, you are dying. What direction is your practice going?

Contribution

Contribution gives meaning to every life. To be genuinely fulfilled, one must meet the need of Contribution. If you want to really live, then give. Contribution is living "outside yourself" – recognizing that life is bigger than you and offering you opportunities to give back. If your purpose in business is to create or contribute something more than your business, you will attract a huge amount of admirers and clients.

So why the lesson in Human Needs Psychology? Simple. If you believe that every decision and choice a person makes (and has made in their lifetime) is driven by the desire to fulfill these six basic needs – regardless of their social status, education, occupation, and gender, then you have embraced the single most important concept to growing a successful business.

Earlier, I mentioned the importance of having a deep understanding and connection with the wants and needs of your patients/clients and your team. If you understand that, then part of the blueprint for your success is leveraging the value of Human Needs Psychology.

So how do you incorporate Human Needs Psychology into your practice?

Here's how:

1). Ask thoughtful open-ended questions.

The key word here is thoughtful. This might sound elementary to some of you, but I can tell you from much observation that your questions really need work. I often hear, "what brings you in today?" or "how can we help you today?" or worse "what's bothering you today?"

These questions are too generic, too off-the-shelf, too boring. Remember, you want to be in control of the discussion otherwise the consult will take an enormous amount of time, and you'll never get to the real reason why the patient is there – meaning that you won't make that vital emotional connection that opens the door to complete trust and ultimately the creation of a Raving Fan.

My dear friend Ava Shamban, MD from Santa Monica is as brilliant a business owner as she is a gifted clinician. Ava taught me the importance of asking thoughtful questions that focus on the positive and not the negative. She calls this approach The Signature Feature™. The "Signature Feature" approach takes into account the individuality of each patient by finding their best feature and enhancing it to become the focal point of their appearance.

However, here is the magic. Ava asks each patient to tell *her* what the patient feels is his/her most attractive feature. This catches some patients off guard and forces them to open up and verbalize something that they would not normally speak about but are deeply proud of, emotionally proud of (there's that word emotion again!).

Even better, since this approach is rooted in the positive, it leads to other comments that generate even more emotion like, "I get my eyes from my Dad."

Thinking about one's parents in most cases yields an emotion, one way or another, and in most cases, eases tension. Think about it. What has that patient been thinking about since the day the appointment with you was made? *Pain? Needles?* ***Botched****? Toxins? Discomfort? What will my friends think? What will my significant other think? How much is this going to cost? Is it worth it?* All genuine thoughts. And all negative. Even if the patient was referred to you, there will probably still be a sense of nervousness, anxiety, and fear. It is natural but not conducive to building trust.

Thoughtful questions immediately ease this tension, allowing the patient to be relaxed and open with you.

Then and only then are you able to make that deep emotional connection that is so essential to creating an extraordinary outcome for the patient.

Remember the entire discussion is about them not you or your services.

2). Listen Intently

You are probably saying to yourself at this point "Listen? That's so basic; I listen to my patients all the time." No, you do not. You may hear them, but you are not listening. Proof of this is obviously in the Kurkjian paper mentioned earlier [(1)] where the practitioners' understanding of what their patients wanted was quite different from what the patients actually wanted. So we are NOT listening. Research suggests that a practitioner will interrupt a patient within a mere 21 seconds of beginning a conversation.

Dr. Ruth Charon from Columbia University has created a Narrative Medicine curriculum designed to teach medical students in part the value of storytelling and, importantly in this case, "story listening." (Charon 2008) They are taught to listen more emphatically to patients' stories and interpret those stories with a great sense of acuity, as Dan Pink reports in his best seller *A Whole New Mind.* (Pink 2006) So listening with purpose is key to maximizing the aesthetic consult and interactions with patients/clients.

Listening as it relates to Human Needs Psychology opens the door to better understanding your patients' most powerful, most dominant needs. Developing the skill of "story listening" will easily uncover each patient's dominant needs.

For example, if during the consult the patient comments about how stressful life is and discuss the hassles of his/her daily life (e.g., getting the kids off to school or hustling them to music practice, caring for an elderly parent, planning a social event), which of the six human needs are most dominant in this patient?

If you said Certainty, you are right; having the need to control every situation at every moment. I am willing to bet that you have quite a few clients with this need.

How about this one: a patient is discussing her anxiousness and nervousness about an upcoming class reunion that she hasn't attended in years. She just learned that her old high school flame is coming too. She shyly shares some stories about that relationship, recounting the good old days. Which of the six human needs is she trying to meet? If you said Love and Connection, you could be partially correct, but the dominant need – is Significance.

Remember that dominant needs drive choice and decisions. She wants to feel special and make not just an impression but a serious statement at her class reunion. As I mentioned before, in my experience Significance is a key need that drives aesthetic patients and the choices/decisions that they make.

Figure out ways to make your clients feel significant and watch the dollars roll in. The Wynn and Encore Resorts and Casinos in Las Vegas are great examples of creating significance. These wildly successful enterprises operate solely on the premise of making guests feel extremely significant. From the bellman to the front desk to conceierge to the room staff, to the dealers and shop staff, fulfilling the human need of significance abounds and so do the dollars. There is absolutely nothing wrong with making people feel significant if the intent really is to make them feel important.

No coercion or deceit here, just a bona fide attempt to help people feel great about themselves. And there is a very high liklihood that they will gladly open their wallet to get that feeling. Don't you? Here is the best part: making people feel significant doesn't require a huge marketing budget or added expenses.

If you and your team can make someone feel significant and important, you will own the aesthetic market in your area and beyond!

3). Speak to the Patient's Needs

You have prepared well and asked thoughtful questions. You listened acutely (without interruption) to their "story" – and you have identified what you believe are the patient's two most predominant human needs. Now here's the value of using Human Needs Psychology with your patients.

Respond and counsel using language and your own story that connects directly with the patient's dominant needs.

If the patient's dominant need is Love and Connection, speak in terms of how you, the patient and your team will work together to create an amazing result – a result that the patient will love and importantly, so will his/her family and friends. Share a story of how another patient, family member or friend experienced a "similar situation" – and how you solved their problem.

Remember, successful businesses solve problems. If your interaction focuses on uncovering and solving a patient's problem and solving that problem in a way that goes beyond their expectation, well, you have just created a Raving Fan!

How much more productive and valuable would your consults be if the focus featured words, thoughts, and stories that were deeply important to your patient and aligned with their dominant needs? If it's important, it's emotional, and it's emotion that drives business.

Imagine the value you could add to each patient by helping them uncover something they didn't even know they wanted or needed? Apple does this all the time with its technological advances.
Imagine the trust you would build. Imagine the loyalty this creates. Imagine your practice full of Raving Fans.

This truly is your time to influence the patient in making the right decision. Influence is the most powerful force on earth – natural or otherwise. I speak about the power of influence a bit later, but using Human Needs Psychology with your patients, especially in those initial consults, goes a long way toward effectively influencing decisions that benefit the patient in the long term and you and your practice as well.

So if Human Needs Psychology works for your patients, how about for your team? You bet! Remember, I said that everyone on Earth makes decisions and choices in the attempt to fulfill these six needs. This includes your team too! If you understand what needs drive your team, motivate them, inspire them through a keen understanding of their specific predominate human needs and HELP them to fulfill those needs? Heck, they'll run through a wall for you! Try it.

More on building an internal Raving Fan Culture later.

Uncover your patient's needs. Understand and solve their problems. Deliver for them in a way that goes beyond their expectations.

Would you have walked by the incognito Joshua Bell? Such a missed opportunity. All because the commuters were in a rush and too busy to take note of the magic in their surroundings that morning.

In aesthetics, don't rush. Take time with each patient. Listen to their stories. Connect in a profound way. Show that you are putting them first above all else. Make them feel good about themselves, and they will be loyal to you forever.

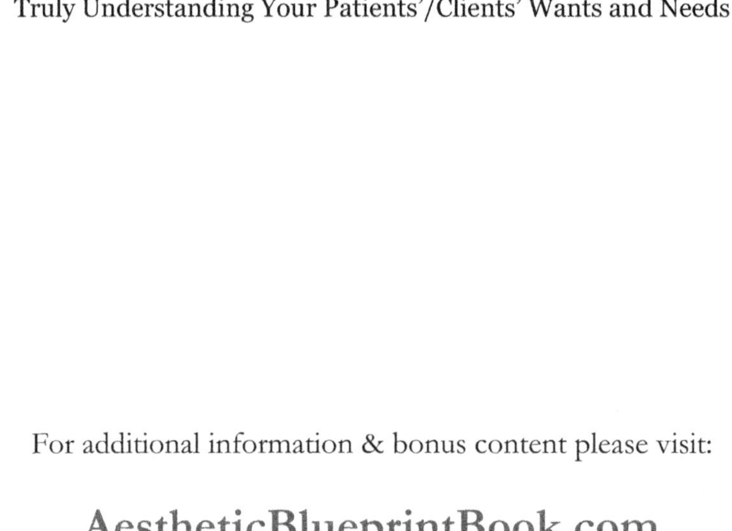

For additional information & bonus content please visit:

AestheticBlueprintBook.com

CHAPTER 2:
Creating the Ultimate Experience

"You've got to start with the customer experience and work back toward the technology, not the other way around."

— Steve Jobs

I was attending a seminar in Dallas a few years back and strangely found myself with some spare time. I decided to catch a cab to the local shopping mall in North Dallas. As I was aimlessly wandering around the mall, people watching and studying, as usual, the various retail marketing approaches by the stores there, I was confronted by a wave of immobile humanity. I am not talking about a line of people; I'm talking a "wall of humankind." So big in size that after an attempt to weave through this mass, I opted to turn around and find another route.

However, my curiosity had gotten the best of me, and once I broke free, I asked a mall security officer what was going on. "Oh, Apple is launching its new iPhone today. People have been lined up since yesterday morning. We even had to add more security to deal with the masses. It just keeps growing." With that, I decided to see for myself just how expansive this human wall was, so I took the escalator up to the next floor to get a bird's eye view of the level below. The mass was much bigger than I even thought.

After all, I've seen the photos and seen the news reports conveying the excitement and hysteria associated with the launch of a new Apple product, but frankly, this was beyond belief. The "line" wrapped around the circular portion of the open-air mall at least four times, making it impossible to tell from my vantage point where the line even began.

Of course, there was also a real air of exhilaration and anticipation. To their credit, the mass was orderly, and all were seemingly enjoying the experience of . . . WAITING!

Why do people stand in line to get an iPhone? With every new product or next-gen launch, Apple fans will get in line and wait. Wait? Are you kidding me? This is a "right now" culture where people won't spend more than 10 seconds on your website; a culture that communicates in short "burps" via text; a culture that won't read an email longer than 3 lines; a culture that won't watch a video for more than 3 minutes online; and a culture that gets annoyed because airport and hotel WiFi connections aren't fast enough. This is a *"fast food, snacking, hurry up, need it now"* culture that comes to a complete halt and is willing to wait in a line all night for a phone.

Let me remind you that this is the same iPhone that can be ordered online and delivered to one's front door. It is the same iPhone that one can buy two days later in that exact same store with no lines. Yet, people will stand in line and wait. They will stand in the rain; they will stay up all night; sleep on dirty city streets; block mall hallways; and . . . wait . . . to buy a phone.

It is important to note here that the coveted phone is not on sale. In fact, those standing in line all night are willing to pay top dollar for that phone. The lure of the discount does not apply here (nor should it be part of your aesthetic practice either – more on that later too.)

It is also important to note that technically some people argue that the iPhone is an inferior product. My purpose here is not to debate the quality of mobile phones, but articles have been published citing the inferiority of the iPhone to its competitors in a variety of technical arenas.

So if it is not a significantly superior product nor is it ridiculously discounted in price, then why do people stand in line and wait to purchase it?

You see, Apple learned long ago that people don't purchase products. People buy emotion, they buy identity, they buy an experience. Read that sentence again and get it into your business core. Understanding this simple principle and designing strategies in your business to create an outstanding experience that evokes an emotional response from your clients is simply the difference between mediocrity and exceptionalism.

This chapter is about creating an outstanding customer experience. It complements and builds upon the key points made in Chapter 1 about understanding your clients' needs. For one cannot create an outstanding customer experience without genuinely understanding at an emotional level what customers want and need, what excites them, what inspires them, what moves them to action, what will make them wait in line all night.

Your goal in business should be not only to address the needs of customers and solve their problems (beyond their expectations), but to give them an experience so outstanding, so exceptional that they want more and want to share with their friends. If you create an outstanding customer experience, not as a one-time event but as something that is integrated into your brand and your companies' core values, you won't have to "worry" about revenue. I can tell you this: create an outstanding experience, and the money will follow – big time! People will wait in line for your products/services too.

It is important to note here that customer experience is different from just customer service. Understand that customer service is vital to creating a great experience, but a great experience is more than just service. In fact, that is where most businesses get bogged down in thinking that delivering excellent customer service is enough. It is not! Not in today's world anyway. People want more than just great service.

With the advent of the internet, mobile phones, social media and more, information and content can be accessed in a moment from almost anywhere. Today's consumer has much more knowledge than consumers of yesteryear.

Their attitude is "Find me and talk about what I care about or I'm not listening to you," says Shelley Pisarra, Senior Vice President, Research and Insights at Wasserman. (Bova 2017)

This is why the old, antiquated, yet still very present advertising strategy of "interrupt and sell" does not work with today's smart consumer who wants information and content that is valuable to them and free. Businesses that recognize this desire and deliver it to their customers are indeed the market leaders. This has created a change in the economy and how successful business is conducted today. Our economy has evolved from a service economy to an experience economy.

First, let's define customer experience. My parents owned a small grocery store back in the 1960s and 70s. My father inherited the store from his aunt and uncle, who had reached retirement age. My dad was a brilliant guy with a wonderfully artistic eye and a terrific sense of "people." Although they had many other interests, my father and mother together owned and managed Bruno's Store, named after his retiring uncle, Bill Bruno.

It was at Bruno's Store where the foundations of my understanding of business were poured. As young teenagers, my brother Dan and I were "commissioned" to "help out" at the store. At first, our tasks were labor intensive like re-stocking and replenishing shelves. However, as time passed and we got older, we were given more responsibility, ultimately being accountable for opening the store in the morning and closing at night. Saturdays were the busiest days, and I distinctly remember those fall Saturday mornings, dragging my body out of bed after playing a high school football game the night before and heading to Bruno's. It didn't matter if I had scored three touchdowns the night before or if my team lost, I was headed to Bruno's on Saturday morning.

Like most teens, I would have preferred to sleep in on Saturday, but my folks would have none of that. I wasn't happy about it, but I look back on it now with great gratitude because I learned so much about people, their habits, and how they make choices.

I have always enjoyed the quote from Mark Twain, *"My father was an amazing man. The older I got, the smarter he got."* In my life, truer words were never spoken, for it was at Bruno's where my father taught me the concept of the customer experience. I frankly don't know if he actually defined it in those words, but the spirit of creating an experience for customers at Bruno's was evident in everything we did. Funny, it is only now as I reflect back on those days that I realize that what he taught me, albeit indirectly through his actions, are actually the same principles that megabrands like Apple and Starbucks use today.

Mind you, Bruno's existed in the era before the emergence of supermarket chains and shopping malls. Bruno's was by definition a "Mom and Pop" store, selling everything from meats to cereals, to shoes, to toilet paper and the like. It was literally a one-stop shop. It was a convenience store before the concept even existed. However, despite that, there were three other grocery stores within a few blocks of Bruno's, so shoppers did indeed have a choice.

Although I never heard my parents speak of the neighboring competition, I knew that they had a strategy that went beyond just providing the goods and services from Bruno's. They had a keen focus on their customers, many of whom were dear friends as we lived in a small coal-mining town in Western Pennsylvania. Their focus was making sure that customers had a great experience. For example, one of my early "labor intensive" jobs was to not only bag groceries but also physically carry those grocery bags directly out to the customer's car and carefully load them into the car.

There was never a question like, "Can I help you out with your bags?" Nope, it was assumed that this part of the experience. Did everyone take advantage of this offer? No, but even if the act did not occur, there was this sense of "experience." My dad even went so far as to offer personal delivery of groceries. People would call in their orders; I would fulfill them, load them into our family car and personally deliver them to that customer's home. I mean that I actually carried the bags into their homes.

I loved providing this experience, especially once I got my driver's license! Nothing is more personal than someone inviting you into their home, even if it is just to deliver groceries. We were taught professional manners for how to deliver to someone's home. Tips were never accepted.

Bruno's had many customers whom we would call blue-collar workers today. These were hard working laborers who took great pride in their work and their families, and usually carried a lunch pail to work with them. Thus, Bruno's sold a ton of lunchmeats and cheeses for sandwiches. My dad was always thinking of ways to add value for these folks.

Understanding that eating the same sandwich every day can get a little boring, my dad would search for and purchase a new lunchmeat or cheese that was a bit different (the need of uncertainty).
However, instead of advertising this new product with an ad or banner in the store, my dad would offer each customer a taste. *"Hey, I just got this in, taste it and let me know what you think,"* he would say.

Never a hard sell or close, just offering the experience of taste. Dad asked for nothing in return. Most people would accept his offer, taste the lunchmeat, comment on how great it tasted and never purchase it, at least not right then. However, sure enough to my dad's accurate prediction, that customer would usually return in a few hours to buy a full pound of that item.

I learned two lessons from this. First, that customer experience must create a feeling, an emotion; something tasting good evokes an emotion. The fact that my dad was giving away something for free did not generate the emotion, but couple the goodwill generated with the wonderful taste of the food item and emotion will flow. This ties to the second lesson, which is that to create a great customer experience you have to appeal to all six senses.

In this case, taste and touch were the primary senses linked to my dad's generous act of giving with nothing expected in return.

Needless to say, Bruno's sold a lot of sandwich items. Whoever thought you could create create a customer experience with bologna? Well, my dad did. Now when I walk through Costco and other mass grocers and see the 'tasting' kiosks staffed with hair-netted employees serving tastings of new products, I have to smile and think of my dad, who would probably take credit for being ahead of his time.

I learned another customer experience lesson from my dad at Bruno's, but this one was a hard one. As I mentioned, many of our clients were laborers working long hours in steel mills and coal mines in Western Pennsylvania. They didn't make much money, and back then many found themselves financially strapped. To help out and to add value to their lives, my dad instituted a credit system at Bruno's. If the customer couldn't pay at the time of purchase, we were instructed to write down the purchase and the amount and file it away. Some people came back and paid their debt.

Others, well, others did not. This drove my brother and me crazy, because it felt like "robbery." After all, my parents had overhead like any business. However, this never seemed to bother my dad. When the store was closed years later, we found countless unpaid credit slips. Purchases that people made on credit and never repaid. Again, that never seemed to bother my dad. Granted, giving profit away is not a good business model but for my dad, it was part of creating the experience, contributing to the needs of these people and a sense of respect and trust. I guess you could say that one of his primary Human Needs was contribution.

When my dad died, a line of several hundred people waited for 3 hours in the rain to pay their respects. Not all of them were Bruno's customers, but many of them were. Many took the time to tell my family their own stories about my dad and how he touched their lives in very special ways, emotional ways. To my dad, their respect and thanks for the good he had done for them far outweighed those unpaid credit slips.

To this day, I remain convinced that creating a great customer experience is not just the cornerstone of business, it is the bedrock for which it exists. In 1998, the Harvard Business Review published an article written by Joseph Pine and James Gilmore entitled "*How do you build a loyal customer base from scratch?*" (Pine & Gilmore, 1998) Of everything that I have read and studied on the Customer Experience, this article stands alone as the best that I have read.

The writer deftly explains the historical *"progression of the economy,"* suggesting that the best way to attract ideal customers is by creating memorable experiences that are engaging to them in a personal way. Importantly, one can charge more for their product or service if it is associated with a memorable experience. Why can Starbucks, Apple, and Disney charge top dollar for their products, for which people will wait in a long line to receive? Not because they necessarily have the best product but because these great brands have figured out how to create a great experience for their customers. Ask yourself these questions: does Starbucks make the best coffee? Does Disneyland offer the best thrill rides for a theme/amusement park? Does Apple offer supreme exclusive technology that no one else offers? Many would answer "no" to these questions.

Regardless of your answer, these super brands have embraced the concept of "experience" to become the market leaders in their respective categories.

Apple Stores offer a unique experience where you touch, listen, use, and interact with their products. Disney, the master of the experience, charges handsomely to receive that experience. In addition, Disney sells more of their products and services to you while you are enjoying the experience.

Pine and Gilmore describe the experience economy as using your service as a stage and your products as props to create a memorable, personal experience for your customers. (Pine & Gilmore, 1998) Of course, the Human Needs Psychology discussed in the last chapter drives much of that experience.

Stroll into a Starbucks on any given morning in any given city and be prepared to stand in line. While you wait in line for your "double shot, wet schmoka-mocha, extra hot" drink, pause for a moment and look around you. Observe the activity, interactivity and the hustle and bustle of that surrounding. Look for the six human needs described in the last chapter, and you will see them in full bloom. Do you see them being met in some way? You should, and it's all because Starbucks creates a great experience for each person in the crowded venue.

There are two key points about taking advantage of the Experience Economy and creating a memorable customer experience. Key point 1: Customer experience is not customer service. Services in many cases are individual and reactive, and importantly can and are being commoditized. Remember: the only thing people care about in a commoditized market is the price. In a commoditized market, consumers could care less about who is providing the service or goods, all they care about is the price.

Hey, aesthetic market, does this sound familiar?

Creating an experience, one that is genuine, authentic and personal, is memorable. Here's the best part, experiences are inherently personal, meaning that no two people will have the exact same experience. How powerful of a marketing tool is that? This is why Apple and Starbucks have been so successful. It's not the products that they sell; it's the unique experiences their consumers have with their products. These experiences create emotion and give the consumer an identity, something that they associate with, something that speaks to who they are.

For many people, being one of the first to get the newest, latest iPhone is a big deal – an emotional big deal for them. Something they can tell their friends and family. In fact, it's so important to them that they will stay up all night, in the rain, just to be one of the first to get the new iPhone! Why do people tattoo the Harley Davidson logo on their skin? Because it's an identity, it speaks to who they are – the badass!

The second key point, and this is really key, is that people will pay top dollar for an outstanding experience. Let me say that again – People will pay top dollar for an experience.

The reason why Starbucks can charge $5 (or more) for a cup of coffee versus, say, McDonald's or Dunkin' Donuts, who charge under $2, is because of the Starbucks experience. Create an outstanding experience, and you can charge top dollar for it.

I bring this issue up here because quite a few of my aesthetic practitioner clients struggle with price and how to charge well for their services. I am told stories like "patients won't pay for this" or "I can't get patients to do more" or "I can't compete with the new spa down the street because they are giving Botox away" or the "economy is so bad that no one's coming in." These stories might be true in your own mind, but it's not reality. If all these stories were really true, then why are some many practices thriving and growing? If your practice is struggling with cost, a great place to begin (besides inside your head – more on this later) – is to create an exceptional experience for your clients. Create an outstanding experience – I mean outstanding – and people will happily pay for your services.

Here's another thought. *What if you charged admission to get your services?* I often hear at aesthetic conferences, the question asked, "so you charge for your consults?" and am often stunned by some of the responses from the "thought leaders". Many of them say, no, they do not charge for the consult, citing a host of lame supporting reasons. Alternatively, there's the fence sitter who says, *"Yes, I charge for the consult, but apply it to the cost of treatment."* What?

These responses just devalued your many years of medical training and the significant investment you made in opening your practice. Just like that, you have communicated to your potential customers that the consult is really just a formality and not integral to THEIR betterment. It's no wonder patients keep their wallets closed. Think of it this way: have you ever been to an art show and only paid for part of a painting?

Does Disney give you the first ride free and charge you later if you like it? The most valuable assets that you have are your talent and the value that you offer. Don't ever give that away!

To be fair, I used to be on the fence sitter side, playing the neutral, nice guy card searching for that balance between charging and trying to secure the client. Like other fence sitters, my focus was on the initial financial gain instead of creating an outstanding experience.

Now I tell all my clients that I coach and preach from the stage, to charge for your consult and all your services. Anything short of that inherently detracts from your ability (and your team's ability) to create a Raving Fan customer base. However, here's the caveat – you have got to create an outstanding experience for each patient. You have to understand that people WANT to pay for an outstanding experience. But again, it has to be *outstanding.*

Here is what changed my mind. Annually, I pay $120 to Costco for the right to buy stuff from their store. What? Yep, I pay them a fee to get a membership and this gives me the right to buy things from them! Oh and I still buy hundreds of dollars of goods from them a year too. Moreover, I'm not the only one. Go to any Costco on a Saturday afternoon with shopping carts ablazin'! Remember, every cart there cost at least $120 just to have the opportunity to be a Costco member to get goods for which we happily pay. What a concept!

But Costco is an excellent example of creating a great experience. Most of us think that an outstanding experience begins with physical aesthetics, meaning the look and feel of the place. For example, walking into a Ritz-Carlton or Four Seasons screams that you are about to have an outstanding experience. Many of you spend thousands of dollars on the physical look of your office, which is great, but know that although a welcoming physical space is a good thing, it does not guarantee that the client will have an outstanding experience. Costco with its warehouse appeal is anything but aesthetically pleasing at first glance, but then again, maybe it is.

Think of the wide aisles that make it easy to navigate, the easy-to-read visible price cards, so that you don't have to search high and low for a price tag.

Think of the easy return policy Costco offers or the tasting kiosks that I mentioned earlier. These are all part of the Costco experience that again requires a membership fee. Do people still stand in line to check out? Yes. Do people still stand in line to return goods? Yes. Do people wait in line to order and pick up a hot Costco pizza? Yes, and here's the kicker – at the very end as you are trying to leave the store with your unbagged items you have to wait in line for one final check out as a staffer cross matches your purchased goods with your receipt. Ah, the privileges of membership!

However, Costco creates an outstanding experience for its target audience. Mind you; not everyone is a Costco customer. Not everyone finds the Costco experience appealing. And Costco could care less about them! *Costco is only interested in creating an outstanding experience for those clients interested and willing to come aboard as members to engage in the Costco experience.*

How about the Disney experience? The master of experience is Disney. Does Disney charge for that experience? How about $100 per guest per day—or more? Of course, there are numerous packages with rates declining with length of stay, but the point is, people pay handsomely for the right to enter the Disney experience. However, it doesn't stop there. No way. Once in the park, you still have to wait in line to enjoy the experience, and while you are enjoying the experience, other Disney goods and services are available to guests at (of course) a premium price. Restaurants, snacks, and gift shops, all products of Disney that you purchase after you have already paid admission to enter.

People will pay handsomely for an outstanding experience.

Even more, people will be tolerable and patient just to experience the experience (i.e., wait in long lines), but it has to be outstanding and memorable.

If you are not convinced that charging admission to experience your practice is the right strategy for you, ask yourself this question: *if you WERE to charge admission, what changes would you make right now to your practice to do it? What modifications would you make in design, procedures, policies, marketing, even staffing if you were to charge an admission?* Sit with your team and answer this question and you have begun the journey toward creating an outstanding customer experience.

It takes courage to charge admission. You're thinking, "this would alienate my patients." You're thinking, "no one would ever come to my practice". You're thinking, "it's too risky." Many of you have not and will not charge admission, even with the knowledge and successful examples of Costco, Disney, and others. Here are two things to ponder: 1) Charging admission works – simple as that. Granted, you have got to deliver that outstanding experience in order to do so. 2) No one, or at least very few people in aesthetics, has the courage, experience and wherewithal to embrace this concept. This is the main reason why the aesthetic market is becoming commoditized. Very few are offering a great experience. "I can get my Botox anywhere, so I'll find the place that's the cheapest," is the consumer mindset. This is the very reason why we see so many 'botched' aesthetic patients walking about. I bet your initial reaction to a poor result is that it must be bad technique, but my reaction is 'bad experience.'

Make no mistake; if you are willing to embrace the concept of The Customer Experience and think creatively and thoughtfully about ways to do this as the cornerstone of your business, your practice will skyrocket, and as the Haddaway song goes, "Life will never be the same." (Haddaway 1993)

I wrote this book because I do believe that the aesthetic marketplace is heading for commoditization despite all the incredible technological advances that are available now and despite new advances on the horizon. You as business owners are missing huge opportunities to provide life improving, image enhancing services to people desperately seeking these outcomes. You spend most of your time and dollars to improve your technical skills, which is important, but you spend very little time understanding what it takes to maximize that hard-earned technical training in a real-world environment – to go beyond a treatment. The issue isn't with the products nor is it (in some cases) your clinical expertise. The problem lies here with the inability to understand, embrace, create and thrive in the Experience Economy.

The Customer Experience in Your Practice

So how do you turn your practice into a great experience? First and foremost, creating a great experience does not necessarily require significant changes to what you already do. In fact, it could be only a few minor changes that can make a big difference. What is most important is that creating an outstanding experience begins with YOU. You as the business owner, you as the clinician, you as the person that a select group of people wants to connect with. Note that I say a "select" group of people.

For someone to have an outstanding experience, that experience needs to be real – real to them and real to you. By real, I mean authentic,and the only way to truly be authentic is by being yourself: your beliefs, your purpose, your passion(s); what gets you up in the morning, why do you do what you do? This is what people want to connect with; it's emotion, and it is the headwaters of creating a great experience.

This is why (in a very twisted way) reality television programming is so popular. Viewers don't watch reality TV to see someone's accomplishments or schooling – boring! Reality TV is popular because viewers are invited to 'experience' the drama of someone else's life and their trials and tribulations. Granted, I'll give you that some of it borders on ridiculous, but for many people, it is entertaining. Today's consumers want to connect with you in a special way, in a way that creates emotion. Moreover, your great clinical training and technical expertise doesn't cut it emotionally. They expect that you are technically skilled; it's expected. However, to really connect with them you have got to go beyond that.

Speaking of reality TV, I have always been a fan of talent competitions like American Idol, The Voice, and The X-Factor. I am still amazed at the incredible unknown young talent who appear on these shows.

For those of you unfamiliar with these programs, these are singing competitions that yield a season winner who emerges as the best from that competition by process of elimination.

The producers of these shows go to great lengths to inform the audience about the personal lives and struggles of these budding superstars, connecting with them emotionally and ultimately encouraging the audience to pick and vote for their favorite. Again, it is all steeped in emotion! Each performance is judged, coached and critiqued by a small panel of experts in the music and entertainment industry. Invariably, a contestant is rarely criticized for the technical aspects of the performance but instead for failing to connect with the audience in a personal way. The singer is coached to "feel the real the meaning of the lyrics" or "show your vulnerability" or "sing specifically to someone."

Ironically, the performances that earn the loudest ovations are indeed the ones that "connect" emotionally. So, despite the novice artist's focus and desire to be technically perfect, what really "sells" the audience is showing their authenticity – their real self.

My youngest daughter Anneli is a huge fan of Martina McBride, a wonderfully gifted Grammy Award-winning country singer. We recently had the good fortune to hear Martina perform live at a spectacular outdoor venue in Saratoga, California called the Mountain Winery. During the show, Martina commented on how much she enjoyed the live performance because she loved the connection and interaction with the audience. She said that even though she may not sing every note perfectly, it is the reaction that she gets and the 'love' that she feels from the enthusiastic crowd that inspires her to in return to give her best performance. It was a shared emotion with about 2,000 fans. "What a privilege it is to perform for you tonight," she said, emphasizing her gratitude for all of us who spent time and money to experience her show.

It was heartfelt and delivered with emotion. It was clear to me that she was living her passion, openly sharing her beliefs, her purpose, and what gets her up in the morning. Ironically, that evening it was evident that she was fighting some bothersome virus, but despite that and the cool evening mountain air, McBride gave a stellar performance. Was it technically perfect?

No, but she gave her all in spite of not feeling well, and because of that, she touched the audience far more profoundly than if she had hit every note perfectly.

Think of any great performance, in concert, on stage, on the silver screen, on YouTube; every great performance is driven by the desire to give, to entertain. Many actors and entertainers in real life are shy and introverted. However, put them on stage, or put them in character and it's all about giving in the best way they know how. Again it is not the method; it's the emotional connection with the audience.

Today, being real, being authentic, being YOU is paramount to creating an outstanding customer experience because for an experience to be outstanding it must be real, it must be genuine. It must come from YOU and why you do what you do: your purpose and your desire to share your purpose with your "audience." Here is an important distinction: the experience is not about you, it's about them. It is true that people do love Apple products, but they stand in line all night not for the products, but for what the product says about them. It's an identity. Did you ever see an Apple laptop with that sharp-looking logo covered with tape or a decal?

Hell, no! Why? Because that logo says something about the owner. A Louis Vuitton handbag costs probably $10 to make, yet people pay over $2,000 for that purse. Why? It's not that this bag holds more, or is easier to carry, or has a safety zipper. It's because carrying that handbag, for whatever reason, speaks (in a non-audible way, mind you) to who the owner is.

Author and leadership guru Simon Sinek says it best: ***"People don't buy what you do, they buy why you do it."*** (Sinek 2009) These are the clients you want because these are the folks who will have an outstanding experience with you and tell their friends.

Be you. Don't try to be everything to everyone, or you will end up being nothing to no one. Starting with your purpose and the very reason why you do what you do will initiate the ideas and creativity that will drive you to create an outstanding experience.

Remember, experiences are different from 'service.' Many of us focus on creating great customer service, but again in today's market, service just isn't enough. It's creating the memorable experience that keeps customers coming back and bringing their friends. As you begin to develop your strategic thinking around the concept of experience in your practice, get creative. Set fear and doubt aside. Think hard about "who you are," what inspires you, and why does it inspire you?

Think of your ideal customer. *What needs and problems do they have? What are their habits? What solutions can your company provide to help them meet their needs and solve their problems in a way that no one else can? What kind of experience can you create that is unique and special to each of them? What can your team do not only to engage this potential customer, but also to create an experience so memorable that the customer becomes a Raving Fan? What nice surprises can you create for them as part of this outstanding experience? What can you do that is pleasantly unexpected?*

The possibilities are truly endless. Get creative. Get courageous and seize the opportunity to create an experience.

To get you started, here are a few ideas that we teach as part of The Aesthetic Blueprint training.

Use Phi

An amazing concept that we teach during The Aesthetic Blueprint Immersion Seminars is the concept of Phi proportions: "The Mathematics of Beauty" or "BeautiPHIcation™," coined by my colleague, Arthur

Swift, MD. (Swift & Remington, 2011) To create a truly extraordinary result, you as the practitioner must first understand the science of beauty. Artists, painters, and sculptors dating back to ancient time recognized that there is a mathematical element to beauty. In fact, ancient Greeks contended that all beauty is mathematics and that beauty is proportional in all things beautiful. Research suggests that there is only one mathematical relationship that is consistently and repeatedly reported to be present in beautiful things, both living and human-made, that being the Golden Ratio or the Divine Proportion. (Livio 2002) The Golden Ratio is a mathematical ratio of 1.618:1, and the number 1.618 is called Phi, named after the Greek sculptor Phidias.

In aesthetics, oral and maxillofacial surgeon Stephen Marquardt, MD pioneered extensive research on human facial attractiveness based on a mathematical construction of facial form, which he termed *The Marquardt Beauty Mask*. (Marquardt 2002) Marquardt and others maintain that physical beauty is hard-wired into our brains and is based on how closely one's features reflect Phi proportions. (Marquardt 2002, Swift & Remington, 2011) One can easily look at beautiful faces and understand that this is true.

To measure Phi proportions and to determine facial areas negatively influenced by the aging process, we teach the use of Golden Ratio calipers. These are the same type of calipers used by the brilliant Renaissance artists and sculptors including Leonardo da Vinci, whose work is rooted in the Golden Ratio and Phi proportions. If you look at da Vinci, you can see how all his works are created exactly to Phi proportions -- from his paintings (e.g., 'The Last Supper') to his many drawings.

Clinically, the use of these Golden Ratio calipers and Phi measurements help train the practitioner's eye in determining areas of need and the exact amount of treatment required to create an extraordinary result. These measurements are easy to determine and in many cases quite eye-opening (no pun intended). We believe that the use of Golden Ratio calipers serves a useful clinical purpose for the practitioner.

Even better, the introduction of these calipers as part of the initial facial assessment changes the dynamics of the aesthetic consult entirely. Graduates of The Aesthetic Blueprint who have used the Golden Ratio calipers in their consults report that patients are more engaged, less single-minded, ask better questions and are more willing to accept a more comprehensive treatment plan.

So what's happening here? How does the use of these simple calipers and their measurements yield such an enhanced patient interaction?

First of all, Phi and BeautiPHIcation focus on the concept of beauty. The conversation is driven by beauty. In fact, Dr. Swift tells his patients, "I'm a student of beauty, and I've learned that beauty can be measured" before he introduces the concept of Phi and begins to measure. Now the focus of the discussion has moved away from the negative feelings (personal issues, fear, anxiety) that a patient brings into the office to one of positivity. *What is more positive than beauty or the restoration of beauty – their beauty.*

Second, did you ever have a suit or outfit tailor-made for you? I am not talking about mere alterations. I mean something that was completely customized and tailored for you from scratch, for your proportions? How did that make you feel? It's a personal and very special experience.

Now the consult has gone from the negative vibe to something much more positive. Now the consult has gone from focusing on a single bothersome area to a broader discussion of beauty restoration. Now the consult has gone from your opinion versus the patient's opinion to a visible, measurable demonstration and assessment of need.

Some of you are thinking that Phi measurement adds more time to the consult, but in actuality, once you perfect the use of calipers and the reasons to measure ("Beauty is in the Phi"), you will actually move more quickly into the treatment-planning phase.

Lastly, the concept of measuring beauty is not widely instituted in aesthetics. It is without question an underutilized opportunity (simple as it is) to create a unique experience for potential patients. If you are looking for ways to differentiate your practice, you should include the concept of Phi measures and the Mathematics of Beauty on your website. Talk more about what is of interest to patients (their beauty) and less about the laundry list of cosmetic treatments that you and everyone else offer.

Have Phi posters made for your office; show Phi on every monitor in your welcome area and treatment rooms. Display the calipers widely. Create a short (yes, short 2- to 3-minute) YouTube video featuring you talking about Phi and Beauty and why you believe (remember Simon Sinek (Sinek 2009)) Phi is integral to the overall treatment and restoration of beauty.

Get creative; use emotion, and romance Phi like those wonderful Renaissance artists whose works of beauty are still treasured today.

Whether clinically you need it or not, Phi measurement and discussions on beauty go a long way toward creating a unique experience for your clients.

Photography

Photography is another fantastic way to create an outstanding customer experience. However, surprisingly, photography is one of the most underutilized tools available to today's aesthetic practitioners.

You recall the old saying *"a picture is worth a thousand words"?* Well, there is a reason why that old saying has endured the test of time. It is still relevant today, especially in aesthetics. Photography can singlehandedly become the most powerful educational and marketing tool in your practice.
I am not talking about photos taken with your iPhone or some inexpensive (or expensive) handheld camera. I am talking about constructing a dedicated camera room designed specifically for taking clinical photographs of your patients that importantly become an "art gallery" of your work.

I often cringe when I see before and after photos shown as part of an "expert" lecture on injection techniques and facial rejuvenation. The quality of the photography is so poor that it discredits every point made during the lecture. Think about it. In just one slide, the presenter loses the entire audience by showing a lousy before and after picture – even if the result was good! To me, it's like talking to someone with a piece of green lettuce stuck in your teeth. It is so visibly distracting that one cannot focus on the points that you are making. Study advertisements created by Apple. Every photo is exquisitely positioned and taken. The photo silently speaks volumes to your gift, your talent and your attention to detail.

What most people miss is this one crucial point: cameras don't take pictures, people do. Great photography is not about cameras, softboxes or special lighting, just like creating a great aesthetic outcome for patients is not about neuromodulators, fillers, or lasers. These are all merely tools used to create an outstanding result. What creates an amazing photograph is the photographer's skill, training, and dedication to the craft.

Photography is a game changer in aesthetics and needs to become the art gallery of your work. It is a 24-7 advertisement of your skill, your belief, and your purpose. Well-done photography should be leveraged to create an outstanding customer experience.

Remember, experiences are inherently personal and no two people have the exact same experience. Just like people will have different reactions to beautiful artwork, fantastic photographs of your work will go a long way to engaging interested customers (and their friends) even before you walk into the treatment room because your reputation will precede you.

I have learned the value and importance of clinical photography from Kent Remington, MD. Kent has a dedicated camera room in his office and has taught several of this staff the skill of taking great pictures of patients. He insists that every patient sit for a photo session, and the results are magnificent. He wisely uses these photographs to adorn his website, his treatment rooms, and his lectures. He uses photography as a springboard for educating and connecting with patients because what is more personal than a person's photo. Kent wisely uses photography and the inherent interactions and bonding it offers to create an outstanding customer experience.

Here's how: prior to the first scheduled consult, Kent gives every patient "homework." Again, this is before that patient even shows up to the practice. Kent gives each patient the assignment to find and bring along to the first appointment a youthful portrait photograph of themselves (usually in their 20s). These portrait photos are usually from weddings, graduations, or similar occasions from their past. You can probably imagine the kind of thoughts and perhaps questions this generates in the patient's mind. "Hmmm. No one's ever asked me for a youthful photo of myself . . ." and thus, his or her experience with Kent Remington is about to begin.

Upon receipt of the youthful photo and before even meeting with the patient, Dr. Remington will have baseline photos taken of the patient with and without animation. He strives to recreate the head position aligned directly with the youthful photo, which he scans onto his computer. He then does a simple "split face" photo, with the left half featuring the youthful photo and the right half, the new baseline photo.

Next, he projects that split face photo onto a 25-inch monitor, which serves as the visual "ice breaker" for the consult. Allowing the patient to see a split face of "yesterday and today" side by side is amazingly telling and offers a unique and personal vehicle to engage the patient and build trust. Often the youthful photo has its own story accompanying it.

This makes for an even greater opportunity to get close to those emotions that drive decision-making. It also opens the window for a more thorough discussion of potential treatment areas the patient may not see.

However, let's link photography back to the Customer Experience. Again, remember that customer experience is memorable and inherently personal. No two people have the same experience and a great experience is ongoing, and that is the key. Well-done photography enables you as the practitioner to continue to connect with the patient. It affords you the ability to show improvements over time. You can leverage great photos to reconnect with patients on an ongoing basis. Most importantly, photography helps you rebuild the self-image/self-esteem of many patients.

Kent tells the story of seeing an extremely shy patient with very low self-esteem. So low, in fact, that she avoided having her picture taken – anywhere. She presented with a "wonky" chin (Kent's description!) and several other issues that needed attention. Even though her appointment was for different reasons, Kent was able to connect with her and convince her to consider injection treatment.

Despite the initial positive engagement, the process was slow, but steadily Kent was able to treat her and visually show her progress through her photos. With each session, her appearance improved and so did her self-confidence. So much so that after several months she appeared at Kent's office with no appointment to show him glamour shots that had been taken of her.

How much self-confidence and self-image does one need to have to take glam photos? A lot! There she was, proud and confident and excited to share these wonderful photos with Kent. *Do you think she had a great experience while under his care?* You bet she did. *Was he able to convert her with gentle assertive persuasion?* You bet he was. *Did he leverage the power of great photography to help build her self-image?* The answer is obvious.

Whether you use still photos for before and after images or are using more of the 3D live animation approach, photography is a powerful, dynamic tool that can significantly enhance the customer experience.

I close this chapter with the Steve Jobs quote that opened it:

"You've got to start with the customer experience and work back toward the technology, not the other way around."

— Steve Jobs

Creating a great experience IS the game. Everyone spends time and money on bettering their "technical" skills, and I agree that is important. However, in this day and age of information overload and "want it now – need it now" mentality, the game has changed. The landscape of aesthetics is different than it was merely a year ago and will continue to evolve. The one constant, the one thing that you can affect directly and powerfully, is the way that you make people feel. *How can you take those amazing clinical skills you have worked hard to develop and create something extraordinary for your patients? What do they need? What do they want? What problems keep them awake at night? How can you deliver for them beyond their expectations?*

Don't call it a treatment plan. Rather, *focus on beauty and the journey, for it is a journey and beauty IS the final destination.*

If you invest time and creative thinking into ways you can turn your practice into "an experience," you will see the immediate and exponential growth of your business. Look outside aesthetics at other industries to learn and model their behavior. You can accomplish what Apple and Starbucks have accomplished.

Just remember: people don't buy products or services, they buy emotion, they buy an identity, they buy an experience.

Focus on the experience first, and then build your technology (offering) around that. Deliver your offering in a way that goes beyond expectations and watch your practice soar!

For additional information & bonus content please visit:

AestheticBlueprintBook.com

CHAPTER 3:
You Are The Most Importance Sales Person In the Practice

"The purpose is to offer something so compelling that it begins a conversation, brings the other person in as a participant, and eventually arrives at an outcome that appeals to both of you."

— Daniel H. Pink

To be honest, I have been dreading writing this chapter. I say this because experience tells me that this very topic is a tough row to hoe for many of you. It is a topic that most aesthetic practitioners and people in general, find off-putting and is not a part of their "personality.". I often hear from my clients, ***"I don't sell. I'm not a salesman, I'm a doctor, and it's not in my nature to sell. Patients don't want to be sold."***

I hear these and other more elaborate comments from my clients in aesthetics when the topic of "selling" comes up.
At our Immersion Seminars, I often ask attendees to describe "salespeople," and you can imagine the not-so-flattering responses I get. Moreover, it's always funny that this question never requires contemplation. The answers are quick and dare I say graphic.

I can appreciate these comments and attitudes because the profession of "selling" has long since worn the suit of deception.

The goal of this chapter though is to get you to think differently about selling. Importantly, it should get you to understand and appreciate that you are indeed the most crucial salesperson in your practice.

As irony would have it, I am selling you on the idea of selling.

Here goes . . .

Let me start by asking a few questions. Do you have a significant other? Do you have children or nieces/nephews? How about grandkids? Are you active in the community, your church, synagogue or another place of worship?

If the answer to any of these questions is YES, then you are in sales. Yep, that might be a hard pill to swallow, but you are in sales.

To be fair, the word "selling" indeed has a negative connotation for many. We have all experienced the deceitful, dishonest, hard-pressure salesperson whose sole focus is steeped in greed and inward, personal achievement. They could care less about you or your family. You will find it in virtually every profession. Thus, the spirit of selling has cast a negative shadow, but is a skill that is most vital to success in business and specifically your ability to operate a wildly successful aesthetic practice.

I was having coffee just the other day with a dear friend and terrific dermatologist here in the Bay Area. We were deep into a discussion about how the business of aesthetics is changing when the topic of 'selling' patients came up.

He was quick to tell me that under no certain circumstances does he sell patients; rather, he presents them with the facts and provides options to let them decide. Ugh. My heart sank. For here was this terrific clinician missing a golden opportunity to improve someone's life by giving him or her "the facts."

Facts inspire no one. No one cares! When was the last time you saw an Apple commercial talking about the facts of their technology? Remember, people make decisions based on emotion, and then they justify it with "logic."

Hey look, your practice might run very well with the "facts' approach, but I can tell you this, it could be even better. That is the purpose of this book – to make you better. In fact, the whole mission of The Aesthetic Blueprint is to take you to the next level – whatever that is for you.

If your mindset is "I don't sell" or you delegate this game-changing responsibly to a staff member (because it makes you uncomfortable), you are missing a golden opportunity to make a true difference in someone's life.

The problem here with 'selling' lies in perception: your perception that for many of you, if you really think about it, is based on a bad experience as a customer.

Almost everyone has a story about a bad experience with a salesperson. These stories contain words like *dishonest, mistrust, deceitful, arrogant, pushy, or more graphically, manipulator, greasy, liar, slick, con artist* and the like.

However, we are all consumers of goods and services. Think of a positive interaction that you have had as a consumer with a salesperson. What was that interaction like? What did that salesperson do to make you feel comfortable? Comfortable enough that you were willing to buy her product or service?

If you are saying to yourself, "I've never had a good experience with a salesperson," then you are fooling yourself. You really are. Just give it some thought.

However, don't think about the product or service, instead think about the interaction, the communication exchange and the feelings that it created in you.

You see, the landscape of selling has changed. Simply put, we all sell, whether you're the President of the United States or a street vendor or an aesthetic practitioner; we are selling. The biggest reason that the landscape is changing is because of information asymmetry, where in the past sellers had more information than buyers and therefore would limit the amount of information shared to the seller's benefit. (Pink 2013) Today, unlike the old days, the buyer has just as much information as the seller.

Therefore, the likelihood of 'buyer beware' dissipates because the buyer has as much information and in some cases more than the seller, thus enabling the buyer to make more informed decisions. This has leveled the playing field, and that has changed the landscape of selling forever. In addition, research has shown that people have a higher tendency to buy something from someone they truly trust. Moreover, there is no humanly possible way to build trust if the focus is on you, the seller. This is why mega brands like Apple and Starbucks have built their businesses on producing an outstanding customer experience where the focus is on creating a deep connection with customers based on their needs and wants. If your focus is on helping someone get better or do better and your service or product helps them improve, then you are obligated to offer that service in a way that goes beyond their expectations. Do you have the right to charge for that offering? Hell, yes.

Here's the same key point again: people will pay for something that they deem helpful or beneficial to them. As aesthetic practitioners, most of you focus on "selling" treatments or the tools to conduct those treatments,when what you should be "selling" is your insight, your expertise, your gift, your ability to either help solve their problem or better yet help them identify their problem (and then solve it).

This is a crucial distinction and the difference between your ability to charge top dollar for your service versus discounted pricing. There are a lot of services out there that can solve a problem. However, few focus on identifying the problem and then resolving it. Think about your own practice. Many people come in unable to articulate what they want, or in other cases patients come in with what Dr. Remington calls 'mono-focus,' meaning that there is one specific area on the face that the patient is totally focused on when in fact, there are more, perhaps even bigger issues that need to be addressed. Sound familiar?

Herein lies the opportunity to offer your insight and expertise to show the patient how to achieve an even better result than they expect. Is this a form of selling?

So what if you thought of 'selling' in a completely different way? What if you took a different approach and further developed this existing but dormant skill? What if you could let go of the negative association with 'selling' so that you can truly add value to the lives of your patients and your team? Would you go for it?

First, let's agree that the concept of 'selling' is vital to the success of your practice or for that matter every interaction you have. Second, let's drop the word 'selling.' In fact, let's erase from our minds the old way of selling, which essentially is gone and frankly gone for good. Forget the negative experiences that you've had: the pushy salesperson, annoying pop-up ads, or just general commercial interruption. Forget all that because it adds no value to you. Instead, open your mind and think about your patients. The happy ones, the Raving Fans, the ones that refer their friends. Think about your relationship with them and what you and your team have done to create it. What are the elements of those relationships that make them so strong? What feeling do you have right now as you are thinking about those Raving Fans? Hold that feeling in your body. Feel it.

Now think of the patients/clients that got away, those who left the practice never to return. You say that it's hard to know why they did not return, which is fair. However, if you really thought hard about those interactions – the "one and done" patients – what could you or your team have done differently? Look, nobody is perfect, but I always find a post-event assessment or in sports terminology, a post-game analysis to evaluate my personal performance, helpful.

Were there some things you or your team could have done better to make the experience better, more gratifying, so much so that the patient/client would have returned? Jot down some of those elements now and compare them to your Raving Fans.

For the most part, what you will see are missed opportunities to use the most powerful tool in any human interaction, and that is the power of INFLUENCE.

Replace the word 'selling' with the word 'influence.' Influence is the most powerful tool that you have in your bag. Influence is far more powerful than any filler, neuromodulator, topical, laser, or energy device. It is a tool that you use every day without even consciously knowing it. If you learn to master this skill, your entire life will change. Mastering influence will create more Raving Fans and will significantly increase repeat visits to your practice – bringing friends or family (and revenue) along with them.

You might be saying to yourself; this is just semantics, that influence is just another word for selling. I can tell you honestly it is not. Unlike 'selling,' which focuses on the needs of the seller, 'influence' focuses on the problems, needs, desires, and wants of the buyer, your patient/client. You have created your Raving Fans because you not only met, but also delivered beyond their respective needs and wants. You added significant value to their lives.

Also, for those patients that you lost, for whatever reason, you failed to meet/exceed those needs/wants. The key word in influence is intent. The intent of a salesman is to take something from you. The intent of an influencer is to give, share, contribute, solve and serve to the absolute best of one's ability. The intent of an influencer is to help improve someone else's situation and/or life with nothing requested in return.

Remember the story of my dad offering taste testing of lunchmeat? His goal was to give first and ask nothing in return.

Influence focuses on improving the life of the buyer who in many cases is struggling to make a decision. There are a host of logical reasons to make a decision, but ultimately people will make decisions based on emotions and then justify that decision with logic.

In my experience, as was in the case of my dermatologist friend, most practitioners want to offer some left brain-driven explanation to assist in the decision-making process, when in fact decisions are made by the emotion generated from the right brain.

Don't get me wrong. Buyers want the facts and in many cases are seeking your services after conducting a great deal of research. Because of this, you should assume that your practice is the last place a patient goes for information, not the first. If you are like many others (and me), all of that research can begin to run together.

Thus, part of your role and your team's role is to help them better understand the research they have done so that they can make a decision. This is where you can make a huge difference through influence. Influence is to facilitate their decision, not to force them or trick them into making it (the traditional closing technique in selling).

Mastering the skill of influence and using it effectively in patient interactions is the reason why you can charge more for your services. Offering guidance rooted in a deep emotional connection will help your patients reach the right decision, and in turn, make them Raving Fans of your practice. Why? Because not only did you help them solve a problem, you helped them identify the problem more clearly, seeing it perhaps in a different way, guiding them through the consequences of not 'buying' or the positive implications of buying your services and then showing them the pathway to getting their desired outcome.

So far so good? Great!

Now, to influence someone you must understand and master some fundamental principles. These are indeed basic, but don't let the simplicity detract from their power to move mountains (and the people to move those mountains).

Building Trust

The first principle is Building Trust (I told you it was basic). Trust, and some call it rapport, is the absolute bedrock upon which you can influence anyone. Without trust, there is no solid foundation for influencing another. Some people think building trust is being a kind, honest person, which is a good start but not nearly enough to move people. Building trust to a level where one becomes comfortable enough to share something personal goes a long way to leveraging influence. Simply put, if you want to influence someone for the long haul, it all begins with trust.

To build trust, you have to care, and I mean really care. You have to connect in a way that is beyond mere niceties, goals, or outcomes. Your mindset needs to be focused on a long-term connection, not the immediate transaction that appears before you (more on this in Chapter 4). Most aesthetic practitioners want to flash their knowledge and expertise around to establish clinical credibility with potential patients. Diplomas and Certificates of Achievement adorn the walls of the office or hallways. In conversations with patients, many of you are quick to interrupt patients with what you deem is a knowledgeable response to show the patient that you not only understand the problem, but you have the solution to it.

Although knowledge and authority are important components to influence, like the combination of a padlock, it must be done in the right sequence. Thus, wielding your expert opinion can only work once you have established trust.

Peak Performance coach Tony Robbins says it best, "People don't care how much you know until they know how much you care."

Today's knowledgeable aesthetic patient expects you to have the clinical expertise, but they also want to know that you care. After all, it is their self-image we talking about here.

Many practitioners take the aspect of "caring" for granted. Of course you care, you're a healthCARE professional!

But that's not enough. Caring deeply about their needs and seeing their perspective is what patients desire. So check your 'doctor-speak' at the door and approach each patient like a friend. If you met someone at a party, how would you approach them? What would you say? Would you immediately lavish them with your credentials? Would you interrupt before they are finished speaking? If you answered 'yes' to these questions, you now know why you are standing alone at the party.

Let's stay with the party analogy for another moment. When you first meet someone, what's a typical way to engage?

Finding some connection or something you have in common is a great place to start. As humans, we naturally like people who are like us. Just look at your close friends and see how much you have in common with them.

One of the best ways to connect with someone is to offer a genuine compliment, and the key word here is genuine. It is one thing to compliment someone's look, style, smile or car, but where compliments lose impact is when it simply stops, well, with the compliment. To really connect and lay the foundation of trust, don't just give the compliment and let it drop.

Try giving it more validity by justifying the compliment, then follow up the justification with a question to create further engagement. The compliment must be sincere and from the heart, otherwise, it is perceived as inauthentic. The rationale for the compliment adds even more authenticity, and finally the related follow-up question serves to open a dialogue that you want with that individual.

Example 1:

Compliment: *You must be a professional interior designer.*
Justify: *I say that because your home is impeccably decorated.*
Follow-up question: *What's the inspiration behind your decorating?*

Example 2:

Patient Compliment: *I see that you really take great care of your skin.*
Justify*: I say that because your skin is radiant and very becoming for you.*
Follow-up question: *What are you doing to achieve such a beautiful result?*

The justification statement and follow-up question show that you really care and that you are interested in learning something from them. Also, if this person has Contribution as a priority Human Need (See Chapter 2), then trust can happen almost immediately.

Frankly though, your words are not enough. Real influence requires much more than the words coming out of your mouth. In fact, studies done in the field of persuasion and influence suggest that words can only account for 7% of your ability to influence. In fact, physiology (body language) and voice (tonality) are actually more powerful influencing instruments. Use your body to connect even when you are not speaking. It has been known for years that "mimicking" or mirroring someone's physiology creates unspoken rapport.

The same goes for voice quality. If in conversation, the person you want to influence is speaking in low tones, then you should talk in low tones. If that person is sitting back relaxed, you should sit back and relax. Once you have established a comfortable connection with them by following their pace, change it to your pace, and amazingly, they will follow you.

Mirroring and pacing are two much underutilized tools in building trust and influencing. Both occur at a subconscious level and can have a powerful impact on one's behavior.

If you are still with me on the concept of influence and its untapped power, congratulations! Mastering influence will indeed enhance the quality of your interactions with patients and create Raving Fans of your practice.

Now here is where mastering the skill of influence pays enormous dividends for you and your patients.

Fundamental to mastering influence is the understanding that all decisions are made on a simple principle developed by Sigmund Freud called the Pleasure/Pain Principle – the desire to avoid pain or the desire to gain pleasure. (Psychology Encyclopedia 2017) In fact, *these two forces drive all human behavior.* It's simple as that. Think of all the decisions that you have made in your life – education, relationships, major purchases, and the list goes on. If you thoughtfully consider your decision-making process back then and even now, you will notice that each decision was made either to gain pleasure or to avoid pain.

Interestingly, most people make decisions weighted on the avoidance of pain (not necessarily physical pain) than on the acquisition of pleasure. This is because in most cases, pain is more immediate, thus requiring avoidance.

In 300 BC, Aristotle recognized this conflicting relationship in human behavior saying, "The aim of the wise is not to secure pleasure, but to avoid pain." This conclusion has been vetted and validated by social sciences and inherently dates back to our ancestors thousands of years ago whose main survival goal was to avoid being eaten (yes, that would be physical pain). However, ironically, despite progress, education and man's evolution, our brains will still focus first on the avoidance of pain, i.e., our very survival.

By understanding the power of these two forces (pain and pleasure), you will be well equipped to help others make decisions for their betterment and yours.

True master influencers – great leaders of our time and before our time – were highly skilled at linking decision-making (or even buying) to the forces of pain and pleasure.

Anticipating pain or anticipating pleasure can be strong motivators in the decision-making process, the impact on behavior and ultimately the habits and rules by which one lives life.

Scientists note that often pain and pleasure occur at the same time, causing a significant amount of conflict and confusion, thus muddling the decision-making process.

As an aesthetic practitioner, you experience this every day with patients. Patients are seeking your services with the hope of looking more youthful and beautiful (pleasure) but struggle with images of *botched results, treatment discomfort, cost, long-term results, what others might say or think*. Again, another long list of concerns, all perceived as pain.

However, an even bigger issue is NOT looking their best and ignoring the real motivation that originally brought them to your practice. This is why it is so critical that you help them better identify the problem, get greater clarity and go to the next step, which is associating your practice's offering with solving their problems and avoiding pain.

Therefore in aesthetics, the key to influence is to get potential clients to associate their most desired feelings, wants and needs (all pleasures) with your practice and the services you provide. Indeed, you want them to associate NOT using your services with pain – the painful future outlook for what life will be like (and what they would look like) without you.

To really be helpful in the difficult decision-making process, you must stir up the pain. This is not to say that you give them grief. It means that you show them so that they can see more clearly the pain associated with a bad decision.

If you are thinking, "I'd never do that" or "That's a shameless way to get someone to do something," then you are missing the point.

Again, remember the focus is helping them get what they want – not what you want. If you genuinely believe that your services can make a real difference in the life of a client, then you must help them see this more clearly.

Moreover, since human behavior favors avoiding pain more than achieving pleasure, your job is to stir up the hurt so they can look at the alternatives in a better light.

Why disturb them? Why stir up pain? Experts in the art of influence and persuasion argue that people who are undisturbed will never make a decision. Decisions are only made when the Pain/Pleasure principle is evoked.

Patients have already decided to improve their look by seeking out your services, making an appointment and taking the time to visit your practice. However, they have questions on their mind and like the survival mode human beings that we are, they have some doubt.

As mentioned earlier, here is what's on the patient's mind:

- Can I trust you?
- Do you have my best interests in mind?
- What will I get out of this?
- Will it give me all I want?
- Do I really need this now?
- Will it hurt?
- How much is this going to cost?
- How long will it last?

These are just a few questions on the minds of patients that indeed can conflict with the desire to buy your services. Your ability to link your outstanding offering to meet their needs will be the difference between creating a long-term loyal customer (Raving Fan) or not.

Again, the way to do it successfully is to associate not using your services with pain – the thought of what life would be like *without* your services.

In December 2000, Universal Pictures released a quirky, yet charming (I think) Christmas movie called *The Family Man* starring Nicolas Cage as a fast-paced, career-focused, self-centered Wall Street playboy whose lifestyle is Ferraris, expensive suits, and a lavish Manhattan apartment. Then one snowy Christmas night, Cage's character Jack Campbell encounters an angel played by Don Cheadle who offers Campbell an alternative lifestyle as a family man living in suburban New Jersey selling tires and married to his former girlfriend with two young children. At first, the confused Campbell completely resists his new blue-collar life and struggles throughout the film, desperately trying to reconnect with his previous lavish life.

Eventually, Campbell becomes extremely comfortable (pleasure) with his new life as a family man only to be ricocheted back to his Wall Street life, leaving behind his new comfortable life with his wife and children (pain). Now Campbell is faced with the decision to choose between lifestyles – both offered pleasure and both offered pain.
Having experienced life as a family man showed Campbell the pleasures that come with close relationships and family, and abruptly having that taken away caused him significant pain and motivated him to try everything in his power to get back to his family.

I won't ruin the film's ending for you but *Family Man* is an excellent illustration of the power of the Pain/Pleasure principle in not just influencing one's decisions, but the energy it creates to take action. Other movies like *It's a Wonderful Life* and *A Christmas Carol* are two other popular examples that demonstrate the Pleasure/Pain principle to influence decisions and change behavior for the betterment of the individual and those around him/her. The consistent theme is the intent to help the characters make the right decision.

Granted, these films are whimsical and mystical, but they clearly make the point, and that is that to actually influence someone, you must be willing to leverage the power of the Pleasure/Pain principle to encourage decision-making. You have to stir up their pain and then show them how you can heal the discomfort with your services. This might cause you distress, but again, if your approach comes from a mindset of helpfulness and outreach, you will be able to add value to that person's life. What a powerful thing that is!

It is challenging to scribe any text related to Influence without referencing who many consider the foremost authority on the subject, Robert Cialdini, PhD. In his bestselling book, *Influence: The Psychology of Persuasion*, Cialdini describes his six principles of influence that serve as the foundation for persuasiveness and effective communications. (Cialdini 2006)

1. <u>Reciprocity</u>

Doing something for someone or giving something to someone with no expectation of a favor in return best describes the principle of reciprocity. In doing so, Cialdini's research suggests that people are more likely to do something for you. (Cialdini's book titled: Influence*: The Psychology of Persuasion* 1984.) Reciprocity is not giving something and expecting to receive something in return or "quid pro quo." Instead it is providing something of perceived value as a gift or offering, and in doing so, people naturally feel the obligation to return the favor. Hare Krishnas are masters of leveraging this principle of influence, offering travelers in airports small flowers as gifts with no expectation of a return gift. This strategy is extremely successful as a large percentage of these traveling recipients make immediate financial donations to the Hare Krishna's cause.

Again the Pleasure/Pain principle is in action here. Regardless of the amount, the donation generates a feeling of pleasure, the feeling of doing something good or giving back, while ignoring or declining the gift creates pain or regret for not giving. Even the slightest form of regret has an impact because it relates to decision-making and influencing behavior.

In aesthetics, reciprocity can be a powerful tool for you to connect with patients by offering them something of value in the form of information or insight; again with no expectation of a favor or gift in return. This is a great way to begin a relationship.

2. Authority

It goes without saying that people often will defer to those perceived to be in authority or those having a specific expertise or experience (Cialdini's book titled: Influence*: The Psychology of Persuasion* 1984.) Nike has successfully used this principle with accomplished athletes like Michael Jordan, Tiger Woods and others who endorse Nike products to achieve peak athletic performance. Nike leverages the success and reputation of these noted athletes to influence the decision to purchase from Nike's extensive product line. Make no mistake; Nike uses inspiration and emotion via these authoritative figures to drive the purchase of Nike sports equipment.

It is important to note here that this type of authority endorsement is different from mere celebrity product endorsement, e.g., Matthew McConaughey looking cool and driving a chic car on a rainy night. Rather, it is the actual mirroring of success from a position of authority, e.g., Michael Jordan inspiring (and influencing) all the would-be basketball stars to greatness on the court by wearing $250 Nike basketball shoes.

This is where your certificates of achievement and wall-hanging diplomas play an essential role in establishing you as an authority in aesthetic medicine. Again, here is where you can leverage your training and expertise to aid patients who are struggling to find a solution or make a decision. Note that the authority principle in most cases should be subtle. You don't want to start a consult by vomiting your credentials all over the patient. No, the establishment of authority is built over time and is a powerful marketing tool that if used correctly can serve to attract additional, higher quality new patients. Beyond hanging your authority from your office walls, consider establishing that authority via your social media strategy, your online presence and by using the Cialdini principle of reciprocity mentioned earlier (Cialdini's book titled: Influence: *The Psychology of Persuasion* 1984.) How can you use reciprocation to establish authority?

Simple – through education. By providing potential new patients/clients (and current patients) with information, usually in the form of education, that is valuable to them and something that they want to consume. This can be done easily and cost-effectively via the numerous social platforms where you can offer free education that is of interest to your audience and accurately represents who you are and what your practice stands for. Sharing this valuable information for free, and not formally asking for anything in return creates reciprocation, meaning that patients inspired by your information sharing are inclined to seek your services.
In addition, sharing this information establishes you as an authority on that topic. The best news is that you can create all this without the need for video producers, newspapers, magazines, radio or any other forms of communications vehicles previously required to reach an audience.

Authority can play an integral role in your ability to influence. Use it smartly and strategically to get maximum benefit.

3. Social Proof

'Follow the crowd' best describes social proof. (Cialdini's book titled: Influence: *The Psychology of Persuasion* 1984.) People are influenced by what others like them think and do and will do what others do.

They make reservations at popular restaurants, purchase tickets to popular shows, visit popular vacation spots, and more.

For many years, McDonald's has successfully leveraged the principle of social proof by announcing the billions of burgers served on their infamous Golden Arches. Facebook and other social platforms promote 'likes' as a way to leverage the principle of social proof. Thus, if a post or video is receiving millions of likes, shares or views, there is a very strong likelihood that others will be influenced to watch as well. The Social Proof principle is the key reason why an aesthetic practice should develop a robust and consistent social media strategy.

Importantly, social proof has a strong connection to the principle of authority, which again if used correctly, can be extremely advantageous to growing your practice. If the educational content you post gets a lot of likes or shares, your authoritative figure will increase (as well as new patient appointments).

4. Liking

According to Cialdini, people are more easily persuaded by those whom they like, since we tend to like people who more closely share our values and beliefs. (Cialdini's book titled: Influence*: The Psychology of Persuasion* 1984.) Said differently, we are influenced by people who have things in common with us. Smart brands go out of their way in an attempt to establish likability. This is a crucial point and a key component to building your brand. The principle of liking argues against trying to be everything to everyone. So many aesthetic practices fall into this (frustrating) trap. If you are trying to influence the masses to grow your practice – stop it!

Focus your communications on things that are personally important to you, where your passion lives. Then people of the same likeness or belief system will seek you out. These are the people you want as clients. Let the others walk away.

Unfortunately, many aesthetic practices fail in leveraging the principle of liking. That statement sounds odd, but it is true. Authenticity is what today's consumer wants, and part of being authentic is being true to who you are and what you believe. You will attract people who like what you like, who have things and beliefs in common with you. Thus, your ability to influence and persuade people who 'like you' will have a direct impact on your ability to grow your practice.

Some of my aesthetic clients protest and state the desire to keep their personal life private.

Of course, that's fine; no one is suggesting providing an open book on your personal life, but thinking of ways to establish your authenticity and beliefs will go far in attracting the audience you desire.

5. Scarcity

During the 2017 NBA finals, ESPN reported that a single fan purchased two courtside seats at Oracle Arena for $133,000 to see the Golden State Warriors play the Cleveland Cavaliers (average cost is usually ~$3,000 per ticket). (Rovell 2017) Excited drivers paid $1,000 to pre-order the new Tesla Model 3 sight unseen, averaging 1,800 pre-orders per day.

Unconsciously, people desire things that are scarce and are willing to pay top dollar to obtain them.

Our Blueprint Immersion Seminars are designed to create an in-depth training experience set in an intimate learning environment. Consequently, access is limited. Although not done purposefully, this creates a sense of exclusivity to spend a weekend with the top minds in aesthetics. As people become more aware of the quality of this advanced training, the more difficult it has become to secure a seat at the event.

Leveraging the principle of scarcity can be beneficial to your practice too. Scarcity not only drives interest and desire in seeking out and paying for your services, but also serves to weed out potentially problematic patients. Limiting the number of patients you see might sound counterintuitive, but it will enable you to better define your preferred audience and provide them with the quality time required to create a Raving Fan who is quite willing to pay top dollar for your services. Remember the game is quality, not quantity. Creating scarcity helps drive quality.

6. Commitment/Consistency

Cialdini contends that people consciously or unconsciously want to act in a manner that is consistent with past behaviors. In other words, they tend to align with past behaviors that speak to who they are and what they believe.

Research shows that people who perform even the most modest of favors for others are highly more likely to perform an even bigger favor later.

It goes without saying that embracing and mastering the skill of influence can and will completely change the direction of your practice for the good. Although influence can be masked in subtlety and nuance, do not underestimate its power and its impact on your practice and your clients. I encourage you all to develop your skills of influence and use them in your daily life, not just your business life but your personal life as well. Replace any doubts or fears you have about selling or up-selling with the concept of influence.

Again, the biggest difference is with influence, you are coming from a place of contribution, of service, of helping others. The focus is on helping someone make the right decision. And here's a key point: to influence someone, you have to be influenced yourself; meaning you've got to believe in the service or offering to which you are directing them.

I often get chided for being overzealous about The Aesthetic Blueprint training that I have built. Granted, I'm a pretty passionate guy to begin with, but in my bones I truly believe that The Aesthetic Blueprint is hands-down the absolute best aesthetic training in the world. I believe that our mission is noble in the sense that we are focused on one thing and one thing only and that is to challenge you and help you get better.

So when people ask me about The Aesthetic Blueprint, I am already influenced and totally believe in what we are doing – even though what we're creating previously didn't even exist. If I didn't truly believe in my heart, deeply in my heart, that The Aesthetic Blueprint can and will change the game for you, regardless of who and where you are, then I could never write this book or honestly answer questions about our training.

As the hundreds of certified Blueprint graduates will attest, this training lives up to the hype and even beyond. In the same way, you and your team have to have the same belief in your offering.

If you are going to influence someone to use your services, make a commitment to your practice, then you better believe in your heart (not your bank account) that you are the answer to their problems, that you can solve their issues, and that the value they get from your services goes well beyond the amount of time or money spent with you.

I recommend reading *Influence: The Psychology of Persuasion* and other works by Dr. Cialdini, (Cia*ldini 2006, Cialdini 2008, Cialdini 2016)* as well as publications from other specialists in the field of influence like Roger Dooley (Dooley 2011, 2016) and Kevin Dutton. (Dutton 2010, 2012, 2014)

For additional information & bonus content please visit:

<u>**AestheticBlueprintBook.com**</u>

CHAPTER 4:
Culture Is King

"Your Culture is Your Brand."
— Tony Hsieh, CEO Zappos

The focus of Chapter 3 is on external influence, meaning the genuine intent to help influence the decision-making and behaviors of your clients. Successful influencing creates Raving Fan clients.

However, I would be remiss if I did not spend some time addressing the value of influence on your internal team—creating Raving Fans within your team. Simply put, this is where the game is won or lost.

Despite all of your certificates, diplomas, training and sheer hard work to develop your clinical skills to the highest level, if your internal team is not directly in sync with your vision and your goals, sadly, you will never reach your lofty goals.

As the business owner, it is your job to set the tone of performance, attitude, and expectation for your practice. The actions and behaviors of your staff are a direct reflection of you and your brand. Therefore, it is of paramount importance that you develop a team that performs beyond the level of the high-end brand that you offer. To do this, you must incorporate the same skills of influence to inspire your internal team to their highest level of performance.

Far too often poor online reviews are not about your clinical skills. In fact, these reviews often positively mention the quality of care received.

Instead, many negative online reviews dwell on poor interactions or encounters with your staff – the very people you have hired (and are paying) to represent you and your brand.

I have had the honor to work with some of the top practices in North America and have found the single biggest difference between successful practices and those that struggle is the culture of the practice. Make no mistake, all businesses have a culture and make no mistake, all cultures ooze into the customer experience. There are good cultures and there are bad cultures.

As the business owner, it is your job to create culture, live it and ensure that your team lives it too. Successful aesthetic practices have created a culture that is lived daily and reflects the aspirations and dreams of the practice owner, who has influenced the internal team to not only understand these dreams, but also to embrace them in a way that they are inspired to contribute their very best and celebrate with you the realization of these dreams.

To be honest, how to build a winning culture is a book unto itself. However, given the importance of culture to the success of your practice and the fact that the skill of influence is the key instrument to refining that culture, I feel compelled to share some thoughts here.

Let me start out by saying this: culture is the game. Culture is king. Without a positive culture, no matter how talented a team, you won't be successful. Too many companies focus on talent, skill, background, and achievements of a potential employee and ignore whether that person is the 'right fit' for your team, despite their glowing resume. Too many businesses flounder because they have the right person in the wrong place or the wrong person in the wrong place – meaning that person should have never been hired in the first place.

So what is culture? Culture is what you stand for. What you believe in. It's the passion for why you do what you do every day. Culture is the DNA of your practice and it is much much more than team building, free yoga classes, staff luncheons or motivational posters. Culture is the passion that drives your practice and ultimately creates the outstanding customer experience discussed at length in Chapter 2. Culture is not a nice-to-have; culture is a must!

Where does culture come from? The culture of your practice comes from you the business owner. It is what you believe, your values – how you want to be treated and how you want to treat people. Successful businesses with outstanding cultures like Zappos have spent time defining and refining these values, which are also called Core Values. Core Values are the centerpiece of any great culture.

Core Values are part of who you are, how you work, and the rules by which your team performs. Core Values drive your culture. Core Values describe how you operate, what you believe, how you interact as a business and as a person. Importantly, well-defined and well-articulated core values should drive all business decisions you make. Faced with any choice, either you or your staff should look at your core values and ask one simple question – "Does this align with our core values?" Based on that answer, your decision is made.

Here's the scary part, whether by design or by default, your business has a culture. In the absence of a well-designed, well-defined and well-articulated culture, the default culture that has no direction or focus of purpose takes over and that is where your troubles begin. That is where your pain lives.

As I mentioned, I have had the privilege to work with many aesthetic practices – some flourishing; some floundering. When I get calls for help from floundering practices, they are in pain.

Revenues have leveled, new patients and referrals have declined, there is staff infighting, or worse yet, staff entitlement, and the list goes on and on. In these situations, the first thing I examine is the quality and definition of the culture. I would say that a large number of 'business' issues facing struggling aesthetic practices are the result of a weak culture.

In interviewing the practice owner seeking my help, I am never surprised to find that the foundation of a core value system does exist but only in the owner's head or lost in a binder somewhere.

They can wax poetically about their vision, their desire, their purpose and how they want to be perceived, but in most cases, no one else on the team can. I'm not surprised to find that the staff has no sense or appreciation of those core values. That's because most business owners don't take the time or don't see the value or need to institutionalize or make real their values and core beliefs.

I often ask my audience during our Immersion seminars to describe their vision and core values. Alternatively, I ask "How many of you spend time thinking about your practice as a business? What's your brand?" Few, if any, hands are raised. Then I ask, "Why not?" The answers range from "no time" to "don't think it's necessary."

If you take anything away from reading this book, take this point home with you – IT IS NECESSARY! To grow your practice to unimaginable heights, you need to build a culture that stands for what you truly believe. Creating a great culture is like giving a gift to your team and yourself. So many business issues can be immediately addressed and crushed in a stable, sustainable culture. Conversely, in default cultures, problems fester and remain unresolved with thousands of dollars spent trying to fix the symptom when the cure is fixing the culture.

Although culture is an extension of you and your beliefs, it needs to be lived and expressed by your team. As part of winning culture, your team feels like they add value; that they are part of something successful; that they are making a difference; and that their work brings meaning to their lives. If you create a great culture, this is the most meaningful gift that you can give to your team.

In my experience, I have found that floundering practices try to build culture with money, financial rewards, incorrectly thinking that money is a motivator. This works in some rare cases, but those cases are few and far between. Trying to motivate solely with money only leads to more problems because money as a motivator by itself is not sustainable. In fact, I have seen it have the opposite effect in that disgruntled employees soon **expect** more money for basically doing the same work.

However, if you as the business owner and leader appeal to their soul and not to their pocketbook, they will run through a brick wall for you. Remember, business is about people and people are about feeling, connection, emotion, and love.

Building a great culture actually begins during the hiring process. Once you have decided on your Core Values (the list should be 10 or less), you should find people who share those same core values. That's the perfect hire. Not their resume, not their experience, not their talent. None of that matters if they don't share your same value system. This is precisely how Zappos, the quintessential 'great culture' company operates.

In fact, Zappos will terminate a relationship with an employee regardless of talent if it is determined that the employee is a mismatch to the Zappos well-established corporate culture.

Therefore, you need to have your Core Values entrenched in your hiring process. Your Core Values need to be integrated into the job description. Your interview questions should be developed based on your Core Values. If a potential candidate's responses do not align with your Core Values, then your decision to not hire them is an easy one. Culture expert Marissa Levin points out that you can't ask someone to come into your company and tell them to blindly adopt these core values. (Levin 2017) How can you ask someone to work for you if they have a different value system?

Find candidates who believe what you believe, who share your values, and share your passion. Hire them, train them your way, influence them to do great things and turn them loose to flourish in your practice. They, in turn, will be inspired to do more, contribute more and add more value to your clients and ultimately to the success of your business. Now that is the latticework for creating a great culture.

What about the people you have already hired without your Core Values solidly in place? Well, here it gets tougher and here's where you've got to get tougher too. As the business owner and leader now with your Core Values firmly set and articulated, you must now reassess your team by cross-matching each employee to your Core Values. Determine if each current employee is the right fit based on the Core Values.

In his best-selling book *Traction*, Gino Wickman (Wickman 2011) offers a simple yet effective approach that he calls The People Analyzer to accomplish this. It is designed to easily determine if you have the right people in place by creating a table with the names of your employees in the far column and your Core Values on the top (header) row.

Assess each employee as follows:

+ He/she exhibits that core value most of the time

+/- Sometimes he/she exhibits that core value and other times not

- He/she does not exhibit that core value most of the time

Once you have completed this exercise, it is easy to see what decisions need to be made. For those employees with all pluses (+) – congratulations! You have a performer that meets the standards of your brand. Now the question becomes, what can you do to influence them to make an even greater contribution?

For those who fail to exhibit your Core Values most of the time, they have got to go. You have known in your gut for a while that that person needed to go, but like most owner/employee relationships, it's difficult to decide to let him go. This often happens with a longer-term staff member you hired in the early days of your business, but who now fails to keep pace, is unwilling to accept change or simply not fully aligned with your Core Values.

These are tough calls because of personal feelings perhaps of sympathy and loyalty, but it is essential to the success of your practice, your culture and the rest of your team that you remove this person. Know too that if you don't act swiftly, you will lose the respect of the rest of your team, for they already recognize this person's underachievement.

The +/- employee offers a unique challenge. First, you have to determine the standard of performance you are willing to accept and evaluate that person against that level.

You can use the 3-Strike Rule that Wickman and many others use: (Wickman 2011)

Strike 1:

Meet face-to-face with this person to discuss any issues and your expectations for performance. Develop a 30-day plan for improvement with them.

Strike 2:

At the end of 30 days, review the plan to assess improvement. Many people here recommend that if performance has not improved, you should refine the plan together and provide an additional 30 days.

Strike 3:

After the second 30-day period, if performance has not improved consistently, then that person's employment must be terminated.

Frankly, I do not entirely agree with this approach. What I am about to say might sound heartless or even crass. In aesthetics, where the first impression in many cases is the ONLY impression and there is no room for error, giving a 30- to 60-day performance plan will only harm your practice because there is no room for mediocrity in aesthetics.

Let that person go, with grace and professionalism, but let them go. Imagine you are on a flight from Los Angeles to New York and the pilot informs you that most of the plane is performing at the highest level, but there are a few things that might affect our performance – how fast would you get off that plane? Your business is no different. Your business should be a high-performance machine, and your team makes up the components to make it fly high.

Remember this: Business owners are leaders and leaders solve problems.

If the culture of your practice is a default culture, having no direction and purpose, then your job is not to just solve that problem but to crush it – destroy it and build back what is most meaningful to you, your team and your clients.

Sticking with the airplane theme, I was on a small commuter flight a few years ago when I was called up to the counter prior to the boarding process and asked a very personal question, "How much do you weigh?" What? Why did they need to know my weight? "To balance out the plane," I was told. Hmmm, this was not the time for vanity. Lying about one's weight could actually end in disaster (talk about a crash diet!). To maximize the performance of the plane and avert any flight-related complications or disasters, the airline needed to have the right people in the right seats. This is a great metaphor for how you are building your team and the culture within that team.

Having the right people in the wrong seats creates problems and without question minimizes performance. To create geometric growth in your practice, it is not enough to have the right people believing what you believe. You also have to be sure that they are in the right place to maximize their skills and performance and ultimately and collectively the performance of the practice.

Oh yeah, in case you are wondering, I was moved to the back of the plane. Guess the airline needed help with lift-off, so the heavyweights were moved to the back of the plane.

Sigh . . .

I am a Biblical movie buff and have been since I was a kid. My all-time favorite movie is the epic film *Ben Hur,* which won the Oscar for Best Picture (and a host of other Oscars) in 1959. Yes, millennials, I said 1959. In the 222-minute film, there is a terrific scene where the hero Judah Ben-Hur, played by the great Charlton Heston, happens upon a practice race track where a charioteer is failing miserably in his attempts to get a group of four magnificent white Arabian stallions to negotiate the track's tight turns in preparation for a major chariot race.

A champion charioteer in his own right, Judah quickly observes and informs the owner that the horses on the team are misaligned and that a mere adjustment of placing the most steady horse on the inside of the team and the swiftest horse on the outside would create a complementary team that could then perform at an unstoppable capacity. Now running in sync, the team of horses ultimately wins the infamous chariot race against the Roman archrivals with Judah Ben Hur at the reins. As the practice owner, you hold the reins for your team.

Having the right talent who are performing the right tasks creates a happy, productive culture built on exceptional performance, unquenchable passion and total dedication to adding more value to the team, to the practice and ultimately to your clients – creating an outstanding customer experience.

One person who is continually overlooked and underappreciated is the person answering your phones and speaking with your clients. Think about it. You have spent big bucks creating a dynamic, user-friendly website. You have invested heavily in social media. You hold open houses. You send emails agonizing over every word written. This is all in an effort to get someone to pick up the phone and call you.

Then here's what happens. The potential new client picks up the phone, excited to learn more about you and your practice. On the other end of the phone, a harried voice announces your practice's name abruptly followed by, "Please hold." Ugh. Welcome to a bad experience.

Alternatively, the new patient calls excited to get . . . to get . . . voicemail! Oh not just voicemail; no, it's the voicemail with a selection menu! "Press 2 if you're a pharmacist calling about a prescription." Hey, I'm not a pharmacist, but if it gets me to speak to someone live and in the flesh, I'll pretend that I am.

Voicemail = Bad Experience! [Tweet this]

All that time and effort you spent marketing and building your brand evaporates within seconds – because of a bad initial experience. Research shows that over $83 billion are lost annually due to a bad customer experience. Sadly, as the business owner, you will likely never know, according to Ruby Newell-Legner, a recognized customer experience expert, because only a mere 4% of dissatisfied customers will actually complain. (Newell-Legner 2008) The rest just, well, hang up. That is potentially thousands of dollars saying 'goodbye' to your practice and finding your competitor to meet their needs.

Your receptionist is the voice and face of your practice – of your brand! The receptionist can singlehandedly make or break your practice. Yet the perception of their value goes almost unnoticed and certainly underappreciated.

Here are a few thoughts on hiring and training an elite phone receptionist:

- **Don't use a well-intended family member. Hire a professional.**

- **Pay them well and train them well.**

- **Hire knowledge. Being nice is good. So get someone who is nice and who completely understands your brand and can communicate it.**

- **Script them: carefully write a script for them to follow during calls. Caution: This does not mean turning them into rote robots.**

- **Rapport is key: Knowledge and enthusiasm are not enough.**

- **Don't bog them down with administrative tasks – the job is to answer the phone, and on the first ring no less. That's it!**

Culture and staff are NOT the places to scrimp on your dollars or your time and attention. Building a culture is the game! You are the coach. It doesn't matter how good you are clinically or technically, if your team is not functioning at the same high level, holding the same high standard, you will never be able to achieve your ultimate goals.

Understand that this is what the upper 1% of aesthetic brands practice every day.

However, it all starts with you. Whether you are the business owner or a key decision-maker, you set the vision, create and articulate the core values and build the culture in a manner that reflects who you are. Remember, culture is a reflection on you as a business owner, a leader and as a person.

Here's the problem – most business owners do not dedicate the time to think about culture. If they do, it's an exercise done with a consultant yielding a document that lives as a plaque on the walls of the break room or worse, in a desk drawer. Meaningful words are only meaningful when articulated, embraced and, importantly, lived.

Creating a culture built on Core Values is more than just creating it, it's living it. You must live and breathe the culture every day. You must hire individuals with like values and put them in a position to succeed as a team. You must influence them to perform consistently at the highest level and hold them to a higher standard using the same tools mentioned in this chapter.

There's an old saying that goes, "You get what you tolerate." Many practices hire employees out of desperation versus growth. They settle for less because the focus is on filling a position and keeping the business going instead of doing the proper due diligence to find the absolute right fit for the culture.

The excuse? *Not enough time, no one is interested, can't compete on salary, or worse, coming in from a competitor with experience and knowledge.* Here's a fact: in many, not all, but many cases, your competition is glad that this person left. Moreover, your competition is even happier that this person is now on your team! Believe me, if that employee was that damn good, your competitor would have fought hard to keep them.

So you hire for the sake of filling a position and what you have actually hired is a heartache, a problem that will now cost you sleep. Some sources claim that the cost of a bad hire can range from $25,000 to $300,000 or more depending on the position. Think of the downtime and costs related to advertising, interviewing, training, and a whole host of other expenses incurred to secure this bad hire.

This does not take into account the related stress and management time to resolve the problem.

If you have not gotten it by now, it's all about culture and culture is all about your internal team and how they interact with each other and with your clients. This is where your business energy needs to be because all of your efforts and dollars to attract new patients or build loyalty from current ones are directly impacted by the performance of your team.

Hire greatness! Don't settle when 'filling a position' because just 'good enough' is what you are going to get.

Hire not just for talent but commitment to your mission, your purpose.

Don't hire employees; rather, create ambassadors of your practice. Hiring employees is a fee-for-service scenario, i.e., I perform a service, and you pay me for services rendered. Creating an ambassador for your practice, however, is a whole new level of relationship, connection, and productivity.

Employee ambassadors redefine loyalty in its purest sense. Of course, they do their defined job responsibly, but it doesn't stop there. These team members are fully engaged and thinking about your business as much as you are. They think about your clients (their clients) and how to create the ultimate experience for them. They come in early and stay later not because they have to, but because they want to.

They strive to challenge each other to be better, yet they are there to support one another throughout any challenge. Furthermore, here is the best part: they become the biggest emissaries for your practice. That's right; your employee ambassadors are your best 'salespeople'.

What's great about this is that according to the 2017 Edelman Trust Barometer Study, the everyday employee is trusted far more than any other company resource and is likely to be trusted two times more than a company's CEO. (Edelman's website 2017) So if these engaged employees are sharing the joys of your practice with their friends and others, they encounter with enthusiasm and commitment, just think of the number of bona fide referrals you will receive.

Don't get me wrong, these people have personal lives and hopefully, you are enabling them to enjoy those lives to the fullest. However, when employees are inspired, they find a way to do both.

Here's the deal – searching for and hiring an employee ambassador is only half the challenge. Once you have brought this person on board, the next step is training them to focus that energy, talent, and commitment to obtain the highest level of performance. I am not talking 'motivation' here.

In fact, I don't think true motivation can be achieved from an outside influence. It must come from within the soul. However, I do believe that one can be inspired to be motivated and that's a key point to understand as a business owner, especially in aesthetics.

Too often I find that my Blueprint coaching clients struggle with this difference. They believe that money is the ultimate motivator and that paying bonuses or setting goals that lead to some financial reward is the best way to 'motivate' the staff and grow the business. If you are in this camp too, here's what you are missing.

I believe that there are really only three ways to get someone to do something you wish.

1) By force and intimidation.
This never works for the long haul and completely flies in the face of any quality leadership ideals. Ask the many dictators throughout history how the concept of intimidation worked for them.

2) With money and financial reward.
Money is nice, but it is not enough in the long run and again it is the long run, the loyalty and the Raving Fan culture that you want to create. People will work for your money and take it for a job well done, but it is a short-term reward (regardless of the amount), and the study of human behavior tells us that it also creates an expectation, an expectation for more compensation often for a lesser result. Employees come to EXPECT bonuses or incentives even if the goals are not met or the practice isn't growing.

Furthermore, if the practice isn't growing, the strategy is to throw more money at them hoping they do more, give more, and contribute more. This is insanity! I have never been a believer in using financial rewards to build a culture. It's like the little Dutch boy with his fingers in the dike. You just don't have enough resources to address the influx of issues that you have created.

Again, if you hire someone whose sole motivation is money, or you have to convince someone to join you with money, that person will never deliver on your brand, will never share your purpose, share your mutual passion and most importantly will never engage with your clients in a manner that creates the high-end aesthetic brand that you want to build. Simply put, you have just hired heartache.

I have come to respect the work of Marrisa Levin, best-selling author and CEO of Successful Culture, who in her lead article published on Inc.com, succinctly explained the three essential neuroscience-backed, culture-building elements that if done well, can create a devoted and contributive team member (note that money is not mentioned anywhere): (Levin 2016)

1. To feel safe. *"I can take risks and not be demoralized or penalized."*

2. To feel like we belong. *"These are my people. This is my tribe."*

3. To feel like we matter. *"Is the work that I am doing meaningful to my organization? Am I making a dent in the universe?"*

"That's it. These are the three things we need to declare complete devotion to another person, cause, or organization." says Levin.

Her conclusion is based on information from neuroscience expert Christine Comaford, author of the New York Times Bestseller *Smart Tribes: How Teams Become Brilliant Together.* (Comaford 2013) Comaford surmises that 90% of decisions are driven by our emotional brain (sound familiar?). Thus, in working environments where no trust from leadership exists, the neocortex, the part of the brain where higher reasoning and logical thinking originate, shuts off, forcing a state of mind known as Critter State. This state can be best described as a "*What's In It For Me*" mindset. An inwardly-focused mindset is driven by a feeling of loss of fundamental safety. It is obvious that little contribution creativity and service can be offered in this 'Me" state of survival.

Conversely, Comaford notes that work environments built around feeling safe in an atmosphere of trust create a state called the Smart State. (Comaford 2013) The Smart State is exemplified as collaboration, trust, risk-taking, alignment of purpose, and strong, open communications. It is in this state where your team's energy and enthusiasm boils over into the customer experience.

It is in this state where an employee who is teeming with enthusiasm about your practice graduates to the level of advocate ambassador.

This Smart State is analogous to a social movement related to some cause. Examine any social movement, and you will find that those involved are extremely passionate about the cause of the movement. They are so passionate that they will sacrifice time and money to see the cause through to a successful and meaningful outcome. Never in a social movement will you find supporters talking about themselves. No, it's about the cause and its purpose. Where does this unbridled passion come from? From beliefs.

Therefore, if you create a vision for your practice based on what you truly believe is your cause and purpose (i.e., like the leader of a social movement) and focus on giving versus taking, then you will attract people (both customers and staff) who want to be a part of your cause because they too believe in what you believe. Leadership guru Simon Sinek says, "When we do something that is consistent with what we believe, we feel passion."

Think of a time that you were working on something that you believed was a worthwhile cause. *How did you feel? What did you do?* I bet you dove in head first, sometimes forgetting to eat, sleep, or even go to the bathroom.

You certainly weren't worried about money. Money was not even within your purview.

This is the Smart State – productivity, sales and profits all increase exponentially.

People come to work thinking about ways they can make things and each other better. Fear of failure is nonexistent. Importantly, staff turnover is reduced, and the need to hire more people decreases because you are getting more out of the current team.

I reiterate that nowhere in this research has the almighty dollar been leveraged to create a winning culture or to place a team into the Smart State.

Make your staff feel safe; allow them to innovate without fear of penalty. Give them a sense of belonging and make them feel like they matter. You have just built a team worthy of your 'best in the universe' brand.

I have provided a lot to think about in this section on culture, so here is a summary.

1. Culture begins with you, the owner. It's about your cause, your purpose, your vision – what gets you out of bed in the morning.

2. Your vision and direction serve as the guidepost to developing your culture. It's knowing where you are headed and why.

3. Core Values are the pillars of culture. Core Values speak to 'who' you are, how you behave, what you accept, and what you won't accept. Every decision made should be measured against your Core Values [Tweet this!].

4. Great cultures are built through the hiring process, and it should be a process. There are no awards for hiring fast. Take your time to evaluate each candidate carefully. Take the flashy resume and

experience log for what it's worth. More importantly, interview and search for the human qualities that align with your beliefs.

Ask questions based on your Core Values. If there is a mismatch, no matter how impressive the experience or resume or how desperate you feel to hire, the candidate is not a good cultural fit for your business. Walk away.

5. Train employees not only in the technical and process aspects of your business, but also in your vision. Communicate the vision, the higher purpose. Show by example the high standard to which they will be held. Give them reasons to believe and a feeling of safety and welcome.

6. Be brutally honest with them.

7. Behave as you want them to behave.

8. Be available to them.

9. Show your trust.

10. Get out of their way.

This last point is written somewhat flippantly, but that's only for effect. You see, in my experience, I have found too many business owners delegating their leadership responsibilities to the office manager or senior partner or someone else deemed in authority. These individuals would rather focus on the clinical aspects of aesthetics (treating patients) than on the business side (culture building). This is a big mistake and often can lead to cultural fractionation. Note, I am not saying that you cannot or should not delegate responsibility. Quite the contrary, in fact to successfully grow your practice, you need to share and delegate responsibility.

Every CEO and successful leader has mastered the concept of delegation. Delegation does two big things – one is obvious and the other not so obvious. First, appropriate delegation frees you from some of the day-to-day process and time-consuming aspects of the business of aesthetics. These more process-oriented tasks vary from practice to practice so I won't go into detail here.

Freeing yourself from these tasks enables you to think more strategically about the direction the practice is going. *Where are we now and where are we going? What's next for the practice?* Far too many of my clients spend far too little time acting in this capacity – thinking about the business direction, assessing the practice's performance, and anticipating changes in the market and competition.

Thinking about your practice as a business owner is vital to continued growth.

The second thing that responsibility delegation does is it amplifies trust to your team. Remember Marissa Levin's third aspect of culture building is to make them feel like they matter? (Levin 2016) Delegation is one way to demonstrate trust and confidence in your team. This is the opposite of micromanagement. If you as the business owner must approve every email or communication sent, if it is a requirement that must give the 'thumbs up' on every decision, if you are meddling in every small detail of the practice, your culture will suffer because all the micromanagement style will never build staff confidence, and trust and the general feeling of being 'unsafe' will creep in like an early morning fog. Smart delegation has numerous benefits to the health of your culture and ultimately the successful growth of your practice.

The *laissez-faire* or hands-off management approach is what concerns me the most. Some practice owners work tirelessly to build the practice to the point where an office manager is hired. Make no mistake; the right office manager can add significant value to the success of the practice. Of course, the office manager's primary role is to manage the practice. When I work with struggling practices, I often see that the practice owner has completely delegated *leadership* to the office manager, leading to confusion, alienation, and culture fragmentation among other employees.

Understand this: You cannot completely disengage from the roles and responsibility as the leader of the business.

Remember, people don't want to be managed, they want to be led. The practice is yours. It is your vision, your purpose, your 'Why,' and despite best intentions, no office manager can fulfill that role because the office manager does not own the practice. The office manager must indeed live the core values and make management decisions based on your core values, but in no way should you be replaced or allow yourself to be replaced as the leader.

In the classic bestseller on business and leadership, *In Search of Excellence*, Tom Peters and Robert Waterman (1982) introduced the concept of 'Managing By Walking Around,' which is described as wandering around the workplace in an unstructured, impromptu, unannounced manner to speak with the staff casually and observe the events and activities of the office in real time.

This has been touted to add benefit to team morale, complement the organization's core values and create a greater sense of safety, which I mentioned earlier. This is not intended as a surprise inspection or to catch someone doing something wrong – quite the opposite. It is to get a pulse of the culture and seize the opportunity to influence the team to achieve even more. This style is still prevalent in many major successful businesses today.

Personally, I call it 'Leadership by Walking Around' because as I mentioned earlier, you don't manage people; you lead people. Semantics again? Nope. Leadership is solely about people. Training them, guiding them, and inspiring them to be better versions of themselves. Leadership is not about your product or service; it's about the people who make your product or service come alive, making it great and desired by your customers.

There are tons of books, quotes, and videos on leadership so I won't delve into a lengthy dissertation. There is, however, one very, very simple common thread that all these expert books tout, although maybe not too obviously, and that is this – *leadership is about people.*

Your team is made up of people. The simplest and most powerful rule of leadership is to treat them the way you would want to be treated. You don't have to be a pulpit-pounding powerhouse; you don't have to be a Steve Jobs-like visionary or Joe Charisma. Be yourself around your team. Be authentic – just like you are with your customers.

Being true to who you are and what you believe is the purest form of influence and leadership.

Allow yourself to be vulnerable; you don't have to have all the answers, at least not right away. For in real life, everyone struggles. Sure, you want to be strong for your team, but showing a side of real vulnerability goes a long way to connecting and building trust. Great leaders connect with people because they are authentic to what they believe.

Don't lock yourself away in your private office. In the morning, wander around the practice. Talk to team members.

Ask questions like, *"Is there anything you need?"* or *"What can I do to make this a great day for you?"* Listen to them and be genuine. If you are just 'phoning it in,' it will be obvious to them. Speaking of which, leave your mobile phone in your private office. Don't bring it with you while 'wandering' around. Nothing conveys *"You are not important to me"* more than that damn mobile phone. Carrying your mobile phone with you, whether in your hand or even hidden (if it rings), clearly communicates disingenuous intentions.

If you are waiting for an important call, then delay your wandering. However, don't delay too long because the culture benefits of your presence in the practice as the leader is of immeasurable value.

Remember, the #1 rule of leadership is "Just be you."

For additional information & bonus content please visit:

AestheticBlueprintBook.com

CHAPTER 5:
It Begins With You

"What you think, you become.
What you feel, you attract.
What you imagine, you create."
-- Buddha

In the chapters within this book, I have shared strategies and tactics used successfully by epic brands like Apple, Starbucks and Disney as well as a few top aesthetic practices that make up a very small percentage of the industry's elite. The good news is that you can successfully adopt and implement everything (and I mean everything) that was shared in the previous pages into your own practice. You too can reside in the same stratosphere as the elite upper 1%.

However, here's the problem. Many of you won't. Many of you won't because of THE single biggest obstacle to the success of an aesthetic practice or any business for that matter.

Do you know what that obstacle is? Let me suggest that you grab a mirror from one of your exam rooms. Look into it directly. Aa-ha! There's your obstacle.

It's YOU!

It doesn't matter whether you are in the airline business, aluminum sliding business or aesthetic medicine. That single biggest obstacle to your success is YOU. More definitively – your state of mind or mindset. In almost every situation I have encountered in my coaching where there is lack of progress or even worse loss of business, there's a direct link back to the mindset of the leader. In fact, in any situation where one is not achieving a goal, I can usually point to mindset.

Change your mindset, change your business, change your life. It's as simple as that. By the way, no one needs to hear that repeated more than I do. However, being simple doesn't always mean easy.

Too many of us get into what Dr. Carol Dweck calls in her book *Mindset* a fixed mindset, which is characterized by beliefs and fears that limit our ability to move forward. (Dweck 2006) So many aesthetic practices are stagnated because the practice owner or leader is conflicted by a set of beliefs that are entirely self-limiting.

These self-limiting beliefs are not driven by ignorance; instead they are fueled by intelligence, or what is deemed intelligence, and most assuredly seasoned with fear.

In my initial coaching sessions with new clients, I often hear statements like:

1) **Patients just won't pay for these treatments;**
2) **People are just different around here;**
3) **The economy is bad right now and keeping patients away;**
4) **My business is down because there's so much competition;**
5) **That one Yelp review is killing my chances to get new patients;**
6) **I cannot afford the talent I need.**

The list goes on. We create these 'tall tales' in our minds to justify our failures or lack of success. The Tall Tales Syndrome is rampant in aesthetic medicine and again is perpetrated by fear. Fear? Yes. Fear of failure, fear of success, fear of reputation, fear of financial loss, fear that I won't be respected, and much more.

Fear is the one thing that keeps any business owner from going to the next level. Fear can come in many forms, and it blocks your ability to make clear decisions, inhibits innovation, and stunts growth.

Fear is the voice in your head that gives you all the reasons that you should NOT make decisions or try something new or better yet, take a risk. Fear comforts you with valid reasons to stagnate. Fear is the scaffolding of mediocrity.

However, fear is nothing more than an idea brought about by a brain that really hasn't evolved in several thousand years. Our ancestor's brains were built first and foremost for survival – the avoidance of becoming dinner for some saber-toothed tiger. Yet today, despite all the technical advances in health and science (and the extinction of the saber-toothed tiger!), our brains remain wired for survival. Thus, that little voice inside your head often labeled 'common sense' is actually working against you. It is harboring your survival by telling you to stay in your comfort zone to avoid pain and discomfort.

The problem is, to be truly successful in today's world, one must meet fear head-on, acknowledge it and still go forward despite it. After all, it's just an opinion.

Some clients I coach so easily sell themselves short of their full potential and to what's possible. What makes this so paradoxical is that most, if not all, of you have achieved considerable success obtaining your advanced medical degrees, which I'm sure that you will agree, wasn't easy. Here's the thing – it's the same hard-nosed discipline and determination that won you those advanced degrees that will help you expand your practice, and I mean grow it exponentially. Said another way, the basic mindset that will propel your business to the next level already exists in you. You just need to let go and let it out.

If you want to get ahead, then get out of your head. Countless numbers of studies and evaluations on successful athletes reveal a Spartan-like discipline and determination to achieve a lofty goal.

You basically can do anything you want or get anything you want if you have the determination and discipline to get it.

The story that I am about to share with you has deep meaning for me personally, because I lost my dad to a rare breathing disorder called Idiopathic Pulmonary Fibrosis (IPF), a disease that over time literally embezzles one's ability to breathe. Death by slow suffocation is hard to watch, and conditions such as these are genuinely heartbreaking. I watched my dad struggle daily merely to breathe despite having all of his other faculties at full strength. On April 17, 2008, he succumbed to IPF. Ironically, our last conversation was my sharing with him the idea and vision of The Aesthetic Blueprint. I think of him as I share this story.

On November 18, 2015, a group of eighteen people suffering from Chronic Obstructive Pulmonary Disease (COPD), came together to participate in a singing performance at New York's famed Apollo Theater. The diverse group of performers had two things in common: 1) they all loved to sing; and 2) their ability to sing and share the joy of music through singing was destroyed by a disease that stole their ability just to breathe. We all know the importance of breathing in our daily activities and indeed the importance of breath in making music and song. Famed British choirmaster Gareth Malone, who was well known for his ability to make unlikely people into bona fide singers, was charged with training this improbable group in preparation for their performance.

Think about it. The goal was beyond reproach – singing in front of a live audience at one of the most heralded theaters in the country. The challenge was immense because great singing requires the ability to breathe, and more accurately, breathing correctly, which is vital to the timely delivery of each note. Most of the performers were using breathing support apparatus, creating an even greater obstacle to accomplishing success. Furthermore, of course, doubt and fear reigned supreme in each performers mind, knowing the importance of breath in singing.

During only five days of intense training, Malone was able to connect with each group member, encouraging them to push through their physical and mental struggles of practice. Some coughed and choked. Others collapsed during attempts to reinvigorate their now barren singing voice. Suffice it to say, doubt and fear visited each rehearsal. However, slowly and surely, with grit determination and positive support from Malone, and despite years of suffering and having the precious gift of song ripped away, this group of incredible overachievers took the stage for a private performance at the legendary Apollo Theater, appropriately named 'The Breathless Choir.' Their song choice you ask? Aptly, they sang the Police classic 'Every Breath You Take' to an emotionally charged auditorium filled with friends, family members, and supporters.

In his introduction, Malone said, "Just a week ago I came from England to work with a group of people that I had not met before and we have put something together for you that I think is nothing short of miraculous." Indeed it was.

Watch their story and the performance on YouTube: https://youtu.be/E2A-nVYhP_0. (Philips 2015).

I share this remarkable story here to emphasize the importance of determination, desire and hunger in accomplishing the miraculous. The ability to overcome what seem to be insurmountable circumstances, both physical and mental, exists within you as it did in the hearts and minds (and lungs) of these incredibly amazing souls. It is a powerful resource already residing in us that very few really unleash. Yet, it literally makes the difference between getting exactly what you desire and simply settling for something else.

Let's examine further. If you have a big enough reason why you want something, I mean your 'why' is so strong that it moves you to take action without pause or concern, then you are halfway there. This is exactly where the Mediocre Majority just settle because they get bogged down in the 'HOW' to do something, which is where all the doubt and self-limiting beliefs live. It's easy to give up when the HOW begins to speak.

"How am I going to do this? It is going to cost a lot."

"How am I going to do this? It is going to take too much time."

"How am I going to do this? I don't have the resources."

"How am I going to do this? It's way too difficult."

"How am I going to do this when I can barely breathe?"

These are just of few of the things that those voices in your head say when you think about the HOW first.

Did you ever experience an avalanche or see one on video? The snow falls forcefully without direction, covering and destroying everything in its path. That's the HOW. HOW is an avalanche of negative thoughts, beliefs, and stories that fall so forcefully and with no direction and it will destroy your goals, your dreams, and your desires if your WHY is not strong enough. This will make any situation seem overwhelming and unachievable, which is when the Mediocre Majority just settle for something less. Look around you and see the Mediocre Majority, all settling for less than they can have and deserve.

Instead, create a big enough WHY first.

What do you think the WHY was for the members of the Breathless Choir? Some might say the WHY was to sing again. Some might say it was to perform a concert at the Apollo. To me, it is neither of these. Singing again and performing were just mere outcomes. To me, their WHY was to get their life back. To not let their life be ruled by an outside circumstance. To take control of the precious time life offers and live on their own terms. What Malone called miraculous was not about the singing feats of the Breathless Choir, it was about of group of extremely challenged individuals, each with their own issue and story, pulling together, and with determination and grit changing their lives forever.

It wasn't about a 5-minute song at the Apollo; it was about owning their life again. It was not settling for less than they desire for the rest of their lives. Their respective WHY was so big, so great, that nothing, not even the inability to breathe, stood in the way!

Understand that WHY is more than just a mere thought. It's a massive shift in thinking that can affect everything, even one's ability to breathe.

When your WHY is big enough, suddenly you can breathe again.
When your WHY is big enough, you can move mountains.

All of a sudden the aforementioned HOW becomes just a checklist.

When your WHY is big enough, suddenly you can do anything you want because you own it.

It's the WHY that will drive you to take your practice to the next level.

So how does this work? Think about WHY you want something. Why will this make a big difference for you, your staff and your family? Your WHY should be bigger than you; its impact is beyond you – it affects humanity.

Write down your WHY and read it out loud. Read it frequently. Write it again. Read it again. Get it into your DNA so powerfully that no matter what happens, you are going to make it happen, or die trying, because it is that important to you.

If your WHY is part of your being, then all the HOW nonsense becomes irrelevant because your WHY inspires you to figure out the HOW. In fact, most people are surprised to find that once they get their WHY firmly entrenched, the door of HOW magically opens to them, filled with possibilities and strategies.

As part of your WHY, add in WHY NOW. WHY NOW creates a sense of urgency, a direction to take action which again is where most of the Mediocre Majority fail. They fail to take action.

Once you have your WHY, do something. Make a call. Write an email. Start to write a plan, anything. Do some physical act toward your WHY. Don't just think about it. Do something even if you are uncertain.

Remember, this is a game of momentum. One thing builds upon another and with each build comes with it another action that creates even more momentum. If your WHY and WHY NOW are ingrained deeply inside you, you will find yourself almost unable to sleep – because your big WHY is now living inside you and damn if that big WHY doesn't sleep. Your big WHY will set free a passion inside you that you have let lay dormant for years; dormant because you had been settling for less. Remember, you get what you tolerate – that is what the Mediocre Majority do.

Next, tell someone, anyone, about your WHY. Let your passion and excitement about your WHY flow out of you. Do not be concerned if you don't have the HOW figured out. In fact, if someone asks HOW are you going to do that, just say, "I don't know yet. All I know is that I'm going to rip it open!" That is even more compelling and attention-getting because once you're WHY becomes your passion, the meaning of your words and the sheer delivery of those words change. People will feel your passion and will get excited with you as well.

I am often described as 'passionate' about what I do. People say they feel it when I'm on stage and they feel it when we speak one on one. That's because I know my WHY and I'm certainly putting forth my WHY NOW. What about my HOW? Well, that's a work in progress. Have I stumbled? Yes. Made bad decisions? Yes. Had to alter plans in the middle of execution. Yes. Welcome to the world of business.

For our February 2017 Immersion Seminar in Palm Beach, I came up with the brilliant idea of providing each of our attendees very sleek iPads to use during the seminar.

How many 3-ring binders do you have on your bookshelf from attending previous conferences? The whole idea was to break away from the traditional 3-ring binder format and add more value to the attendee experience by enabling them to navigate through the presentations electronically, easily take notes, and bring the stage right to their seat.

We hired an agency from the UK who specialized in advanced conference technology and built a customized app for The Aesthetic Blueprint. This app was user-friendly and did about everything, including viewing slides up close, electronic note taking that could be emailed to a personal account, paperless CME testing and evaluation, posting thoughts and opinions in real time on social media, and even communicating electronically with other attendees during the seminar. The app did everything except take food orders in advance of lunch!

My team worked so hard to design the app and coordinating between California and London required commitment. We had worked closely with the seminar venue hotel and were assured that the WiFi there could accommodate the massive demand of more than 100 iPads simultaneously. We tested and retested the app – both in advance of the seminar and onsite in Florida. All systems were 'go.'

At registration, there was an air of added excitement as each attendee was assigned their personal iPad. Talk about creating a unique experience; I thought we were on our way. Then, much to my chagrin, well to be honest much more than my chagrin . . . the hotel WiFi failed, rendering half of the iPads completely ineffective and the others only modestly functional. Very few of the attendees had the luxury of truly enjoying the value of that wonderful app. Worse than that, the now non-usable iPads became a distraction.

Unfortunately, we had no viable back-up plan. To their credit, our attendees were gracious and understandably but rightfully critical of our attempt to upgrade the experience. In fact, some gave 'encouragement' not to abandon the concept at all, just fix the "f—ing" WiFi. My team who worked so hard to create the app was extremely disappointed, and of course, they had to incur the frustration of the attendees in real time.

However, despite the disappointment, they were not devastated. Not even close. That is because they understand and live our WHY.

Having your WHY passionately within you does not guarantee that everything you do or every idea you have will execute flawlessly. Not even close.

However, what a WHY does do is keep you focused and unbowed by temporary setbacks, and believe me you will have temporary setbacks – like lousy WiFi!

And here's the best part, those setbacks are actually growth opportunities. Many will call it failure, but with a strong WHY in place, these setbacks are opportunities to get better and better. Some people don't like negative feedback. Frankly, neither do I, but I love the fact that someone took the time to share that feedback so that I can learn outright. I can make adjustments, and I can get better. After all, it's about getting better every day. Again, not learning from these setbacks is the thing that forces the Mediocre Majority into . . . well . . . mediocrity.

Your WHY is built on your belief system about what the world should be. Your WHY creates an unbridled passion in you that drives you every day. Passion comes when you are doing something that aligns perfectly with your belief system.

Most stress (if not all stress) comes from doing something that is not consistent with your belief system. In other words, your work and your WHY are misaligned. You either need to change your WHY or change your work to complement your WHY.

With a big enough WHY, your ideas of HOW will flow in. With a big enough WHY, you will notice a physical change in the way you carry yourself, your language patterns and your interaction with others.

It took me a long time to recognize and understand this notion. In fact, The Aesthetic Blueprint was born out of this epiphany. For years, I had been working my ass off for all the wrong reasons.

My frustration was somewhat placated by a paycheck, but in hindsight there wasn't enough money or success in the world that would have made me fulfilled — simply because I was working with (and tolerating) a weak WHY. However, there was something more.

There was an entrepreneurship in me that was intolerant of my unenthusiastic commitment to the corporate infantry. In addition, the ideas that I had were nothing more than ideas that demanded my full attention in order to become reality. These ideas could only be born out of my passion for bringing them to life.

I toyed with the idea longer than I care to mention. I felt the fear of going out on my own. I had those same voices telling me why I could not or should not do it. Worse yet, I had real voices, those of people who genuinely cared for me, saying I should not leave the corporate world, filling my head with their own crappy stories.

Make note, out of their love for you, close friends and family can be the biggest obstacle to your growth – to your journey to becoming your very best.

I say this not to suggest that you divorce yourself from their connection, but just be aware that what you are embarking upon makes them fearful too. It invites them to unknowingly cast their fears upon you disguised as advice. Love them with all your heart, but don't ever let them dictate or control or define your WHY.

With best intentions, friends and family don't want to see you struggle and (in their opinion) fail. They want you to be happy and comfortable. Comfort is very alluring but it will never ever, ever help you grow.

Like any living thing on planet Earth, if you are not growing, you are dying, and to grow you need resistance. Like a bodybuilder develops muscle by the resistance of heavy weights, so must we as business owners experience resistance in order to grow. Some call resistance failure, but as I said before, if you're WHY is big and living within you, failure is just an opinion.

You see, comfort despises resistance. Comfort says, "hit the snooze button," "forget the gym," "eat that half gallon of ice cream," or "take a break and waste precious free time on social media."

Once I figured this out, a whole new world opened to me professionally. I found a hunger in me that had long been silenced by the 'common sense' of a steady income. However, to make a change requires a change in routine. For it is our routines that create comfort. To grow, you must break out of your comfortable routine and 'safe harbor.' Breaking routine is where growth happens. Some of us have great daily routines, others not so much. In many cases, you can just look at a person and guess that person's routine. Remember that to grow, you have got to change your routine.

Here are some routines that I have embraced and that have worked for me as I've built and continue to build my business (and my life).

Build Your Brain

I start every day by learning something new or different. It can be anything like reading a book, listening to an audio recording, or listening/watching a TED talk, which is my personal favorite. TED talks are normally 15-18 minutes' in duration and you can get a lot of information and insight in a very short period of time. My personal favorites are the talks that are somewhat counterintuitive to my current way of thinking. I find them inspiring and thought-provoking. Such information is great in the morning when your mind is still unclogged from the "LDLs of the day."

It puts you immediately into a 'can do' or 'what's possible' mindset. No, it doesn't have to be related to aesthetics or even business, just find something that is of interest to you. I actually find myself looking at TED talks throughout the day. My gym instructor would call this my 'active rest.' Learning is growing and if you are not growing, you are dying. **Take note: Reading the newspaper or any news feed will NOT build your mind.**

In fact, it has the opposite effect. I stopped watching the news over a year ago, especially the over-sensationalized 10 o'clock news before going to bed. The news media can make a 2-day heat wave in the Bay Area sound like the apocalypse. Today's news media (sadly disguised as journalism) thrives on bad news and the sensational. Why? Because bad news sells advertising. That's it.

The Mediocre Majority want to wallow in their own despair, so today's news media piles on the sadness and misery so that you'll buy a new mattress. Stop watching the news! If it's important enough, you'll find out about it.

Recently, the hot news was the solar eclipse. I didn't even know about it until that day. My point is this; there is a direct link to what you put into your mind and how it affects you mentally and physically. So for you to make the big decisions as a business owner, creating geometric growth in your practice, your mindset needs to be a growth mindset – a 'can do, no matter what' attitude. The media magnifies the woes of the world, although real and important, with a purpose of doing nothing more than selling you something.

I have learned to spend my time boldly looking ahead, getting inspired by the great accomplishments of others and figuring out ways to put their lessons into my every day practice of living and growing.

Build your brain every day for just 30 minutes and feel the wonderful impact it will have on your day, your business and your life.

Build Your Body

Your mindset is controlled by your physical state. Your ability to take charge in a crisis, make key decisions, and show up for your staff and clients all starts with your physical condition. Think about it; when we want to change our mental state we start with changing our physical state. For example, alcohol changes our mental state via changes to our body, so does food and some drugs.

Getting 'high' is an outcome of changes to our physical state. Granted, these are all rather negative examples of mental state changes, but they are real, wouldn't you agree? If so, then you'll agree that positive physical change will impact the mental state as well.

If you are not committed to some form of physical activity at least five days a week, you will struggle with the mental challenges you face to take your business to the next level.

For me, getting to the gym is always a hassle and once my day starts – forget it! Just too much to do. That's why I'm up at 4:15am every day and in the gym by 5:30am. I have a personal trainer on Monday and Wednesday and do class-based training that is a combination of weight lifting and cardio the other days. Within an hour's time, my blood is pumping through my body and so are new ideas in my head. I can't wait to get the day started. Mind you, most people are still asleep or hitting that snooze button.

Here's an interesting observation – on those rare days that I don't work out, I miss it and my physical being feels sluggish.

There are many published articles that support the notion of frequent exercise, but to me it's less about the physical activity (albeit important) and more about me living up to my WHY.

Because it's my WHY that gets me up before the sun and pretty much before the rest of the Bay Area. It's not my keen sense to do squats or burpees at 6am. It's because I have a big enough WHY that inspires me and drives me to get out of bed and work out. It's not about looking 'ripped' (although that would be cool!), it's about showing up for my team and my clients (you) at my absolute level best or as Tiger Woods would say "Bring my A-Game."

I know in my heart of hearts that without a good workout, for me, there is no A-Game. I'm willing to bet that for most of you it's the same thing. Look, you don't have to beat yourself up or hit it so hard that you can't move by 3pm. Taking a brisk walk will do the trick. In fact, some days, I'll combine my body and my mind training together. It's my favorite thing to do. I have the good fortune to live in beautiful Los Altos, California, a wonderful community on the perimeter of the Silicon Valley. The climate is moderate to say the least and the topography of the area can be described as 'hilly.'

I love to take advantage of the climate and hills by listening to some educational/inspirational audio programming while I climb – the best of both worlds! At the end of the exercise, I've met my body challenge and added more to my mind's database. The point is doing something, anything that fits you physically, but DO SOMETHING! And do it every day. If your WHY is big enough, you'll get what I'm saying here.

Drink plenty of water. Studies show that dehydration is a major contributor to loss of focus, fatigue, drops in energy, and much more. Many experts say that one must consume up to 75% of one's body weight daily in ounces: [Your body weight in pounds] x 0.75 = [No. of ounces of water that you should drink daily]. However, if you are like me, something as easy as drinking a glass of water is easily forgotten among the other day's activities that distract my focus. I simply forget to drink.

Here's the issue, if you find yourself thirsty, you are already dehydrated. So to remind myself to drink and keep hydrated and on top of my game, I use an app on my phone called Water Alert. It's free and among other things provides reminders (that you preprogram) directly from your phone to drink water. You can track your progress and keep records of your consumption.

It's a great little app that helps keep you in tune with your need to take care of your body by drinking ample amounts water. One final thought on drinking water. When I moved to California, I noticed that almost every restaurant served water with lemon. It must be a California thing I thought, but I've since come to realize the benefits of alkalizing and keep the pH in your body normal versus becoming acidic. Although the topic is controversial, I have personally found the benefits to alkalizing and encourage you to explore this research.

Take Cold Showers

OK, now you're thinking "Bob has lost his mind." But hear me out. In keeping with my morning TED talk ritual mentioned previously, one morning I found myself, sleepy-eyed and in need something different – not another business or leadership talk, not another metaphysical presentation, I just wanted something different. As I scanned the TED topic list, I came across what I thought was an interesting title: *How Cold Showers Can Change Your Life* by ultra marathon runner and triathlete Joel Runyon, founder of IMPOSSIBLE, a company dedicated to helping people push their limits and do impossible things. (Runyon 2013)

I had been learning the value of cryotherapy and had done several treatments with very impressive results. Mistakenly, I thought Runyon's talk related to the well-studied health benefits that 'cold' can offer. (Runyon 2013) However, the talk was way more powerful and beneficial than that. Runyon's talk was so aligned with the challenges I was facing as a business owner that that morning I adopted his strategy and have been doing ever since.

The essence of the cold shower approach is directly facing something that makes us uncomfortable. I mean no one in his right mind hops out of a warm bed, pulls off warm PJs and cranks the shower to COLD. That would be very uncomfortable, and most people are afraid to be uncomfortable. Even with the best intentions, you will stand naked in the shower stall rifling through a litany of reasons, stories and excuses of why taking a cold shower for 5 minutes is a really dumb idea.

Many of you will convince yourself to take the easier, more comfortable path of a hot shower, coming up with a host of common-sense reasons why not to take a cold shower.

In fact, your first instinct is to turn the knob to 'HOT.' But turning that knob to 'COLD' (and I mean completely to "COLD") forces you to push through the doubts and discomfort an extremely cold shower presents. Truth be told, these are the same stories, doubts and fears that are holding you back from going to that next level with your business.

The metaphor of selecting between a hot or cold shower is that you have a choice – comfortable (hot) or uncomfortable (cold) – but as Runyon says, it is a choice.

You can either believe those stories and excuses that hold you back (hot and comfortable) or you can decide that none of that matters and pushing through any discomfort (cold) will yield far better results.

What Joel said next spoke truth to me in the early hours of that morning. He said, "If you are not willing or able to be the type of person that is willing to be uncomfortable for five minutes alone in the shower, where the only negative outcome is you being cold for five minutes and the only person affected by that decision is you, then how will you ever have the strength or the courage to choose to be uncomfortable in a situation where the outcomes are much, much greater and the people affected by your decision far outnumber just yourself." That did it for me, and it should do it for you too.

As business owners, we are faced with uncomfortable situations all the time – needing to make tough decisions, many of which are uncomfortable to make.

However, if you've already prepared your body and your mind to push through what is uncomfortable, push past your fears, your anxiety and your doubts, push through them to obtain your desired outcome, you will find yourself in extremely rare company.

This is where the upper 1% resides. You see, in my mind, those who are living their dream, having the results they desire, look at what is uncomfortable, what is challenging, and perhaps what others deem impossible and *do it any way.* Every great athlete, great actor, great entrepreneur, or even every avid singer struck down by COPD has faced what seemed impossible, faced the fear of failure and the discomfort of trial, and pushed through it regardless of the consequence.

Impossible is really just an opinion. That statement can be seen in everyday life. Spectacular efforts by everyday people.
In reality, when it comes to mindset, the intense desire to push past fears and doubts is anything but 'everyday.' These people may not be celebrities or famous names, but their accomplishments are mighty.

You too can live in this rare stratosphere, but you have to be willing to show up at your best when things are the most uncomfortable.

Prepare yourself for the uncomfortable. Start each morning with a cold shower.

Get A Coach

About 15 years ago, I was presented with the opportunity to hire a personal coach. After a few initial free initial sessions, I was intrigued and found value, but in my mind I couldn't come to grips with the belief that I need support. Who, me? I was formidable, invincible in my own mind. I didn't need to speak with someone weekly about my 'progress.' I justified this belief with the story that it cost too much and I walked away knowing deep down that I was making a mistake. Fast-forward a few years and as part of an entrepreneur business-training package, I was exposed to coaching again. However, this time, circumstances encouraged me to give it another go and I am so glad that I did.

The first thing I came to realize is that a business/life coach is no different than any other coach, whether it be a sports coach, acting coach, or flight or cooking instructor. The role (if the coach is really good) is to help guide your growth and progress. The role of the coach is to hold you accountable to the commitments that you make to grow —plain and simple. For it is the commitment and determination to complete a task or "doing what we say we're going to do" that creates growth. A great coach helps you think through challenges and work past obstacles that often sidetrack us just because our focus wanes.

It is not a question of mental toughness, which is what prevented me from working with a coach so many lost years ago; it's a question of focus and staying true to yourself and your plan. A great coach challenges your thinking so that in the end YOU create and own the result, not the coach. This is the biggest distinction between a coach and a consultant. A lot of you hire consultants to solve problems, and they do. However, their solutions are often unsustainable because the owner (you) is not emotionally invested in the process, you just want the result. Remember, anything good comes from emotion. A great coach, on the other hand, coaches you through a thinking process, asking questions that help you get over some subtle and not so subtle obstacles that are keeping you from achieving your goal. A great coach helps you see what you don't see.

If you are like me, when you are pushing forward or faced with a challenge, the tendency is to focus on the immediate 'what's in front of you' with no attention for the bigger picture. It's like driving at night in a snowstorm. If your focus goes to the immediate front of the car, the hurried snowflakes dancing around your headlights blind you. However, if you shift your focus to beyond what's immediate, turning down your 'high beams,' you see the road ahead, and even though it's snow-filled too, you can successfully navigate forward. A great coach not only helps you shift your focus, but also encourages you to find a solution. At the end of the day, it's YOU getting your result through a process that YOU developed. That is the most fulfilling result of all – the one that came from your total commitment and investment of time, emotion, and energy.

Growing up, I always wanted to be a professional coach. I wanted to be the head coach of a successful sports team, which is one of the reasons I became a teacher.

Back then, the fastest way to becoming a coach was by being on staff at the local high school. The team sports that I loved were football and basketball. I played both in high school, and then I played football in college. After receiving my degree in education, I spent the next four years teaching at the local high school and coaching football and basketball. It was a considerable time commitment for very little pay.

One of my fellow assistants and I figured out that with our 'bloated' coaching salaries we were making less than a dollar per hour. To me though that was not relevant at the time because I was finally doing what I wanted to do – coach. I believed my mission back then was to make a positive impact on those young men by sharing with them all I had learned . . . And I did.

As I looked back on my sports coaching career, I have come to realize that the role of a business coach is no different. A coach of a football team cannot come off the sidelines and play the game. All the coach can do is prepare his team for the game. Understand the circumstances and obstacles that the opponent presents and help his team find a way to overcome them and become victorious.

A few years ago, my good friend Don Naumann, owner of Sierra Pacific Turf Supply, invited me to work as a volunteer for the United States Open Golf Tournament at the spectacular Olympic Club near San Francisco. Don's company services all of the golf courses in California with turf and grass supplies, so he had an 'in' with the US Golf Association and the head superintendent at the Olympic Club. I was assigned the job of grooming and maintaining the practice tee or range where, at any given time, a host of players was there practicing their craft. Although my assignment and related tasks were somewhat menial (smart superintendent), it gave me full access up close and personal to these amazing athletes. It was five days of getting up early and going to bed late, but I enjoyed the experience that taught me three critical things about the business of golf.

First, professional golfers are incredible athletes capable of hitting shots with unbelievable accuracy, and I mean real precision. They know the exact distance and ball flights of each shot and are able to modify the direction and flight with slight changes in the swing. This precision can only come from practice, more practice and even more practice. To me, golf is a sport, a short hiatus from my typical day, but to these players, it's a living. It's how they feed their families, and their undeniable dedication to honing their craft should be appreciated by any business owner.

The second lesson I learned is that each player is a brand. His dress, his demeanor, his interactions with the media, fans, and organizers are all part of his brand.

Unlike a team sport where players perform under the team's brand, professional golfers are a lone brand, and those brands have varied perceptions not necessarily based on victories. As I write this, the one player that stands out the most to me is Ricky Fowler, who to date has flirted with, yet has never won, a highly sought-after Major win.

However, Fowler has built a huge following and an impressive brand. He is incredibly accessible, friendly with fans and the media, demonstrates undeniable sportsmanship, and always stylishly dressed in bright colors by his sponsor Puma. Despite his lack of big wins, fans follow him around, wildly cheering his every shot. When he wins a Major, which I predict he will soon, his already popular brand will skyrocket even further because everyone loves a champion whom they can connect with, who is real and authentic – that's Ricky Fowler's brand.

The third and probably most impressive lesson I learned is that each one of these professional golfers had a coach. In some cases, more than one coach. In speaking with one of the caddies, I learned that there was a swing coach whose job was to look for even the minutest flaws in the swing that could cause a dramatic erroneous ball flight. There was the putting coach who assisted the player in refining the putting stroke once on the green. Most golf tournaments, especially the Majors, are won and lost to putting. There was also a psychology coach.

Golf is a game of strategy, navigating around obstacles and perils set forth by the golf course and Mother Nature. It requires deep thought and a clear mind to create deep thought.

The psychology or mind coach, as I call him, helps each player unclutter their mind of fear and doubt because no shot can be hit with surgical precision if shrouded in doubt.

What I learned is that even the best in the world, the very best in the world, have a coach and in some cases, more than one coach. Every Academy Award-winning actor, Emmy Award-winning performer, professional golfer, chef, tennis player, has a coach. So why not you? Why shouldn't you take advantage of another set of eyes watching for the proverbial 'flaws in your swing'? Why shouldn't you have someone who can see what you can't see to help you to push through and perform with that same surgical precision? Make no mistake; it's the same precision that all the great strive to obtain.

Moreover, it is the same precision that every aesthetic practitioner should seek too, but it cannot be done alone. Nothing great can be done alone. Great coaches push to the next level. Great coaches eliminate self-doubt and pity because there is no room for these at the next level.

My coach helped me see that there was so much more potential in my business and in me as a person and we have been working together to get to my next level. That feeling of success and the realization that I can't get there alone is why I now offer my coaching services to select clients.

Getting a coach is hands-down the smartest decision I have made in the past five years. Thanks, Ricky.

Get New Friends

I recently attended a business conference designed for entrepreneurs from across the country and a few outside the US.

The 2-day event featured presentations from successful entrepreneurs like Jeff Hoffman, Co-Founder of Priceline; Brian Smith, Founder of Ugg Boots; Tom Bilyeu, Co-Founder of Quest Nutrition; and renowned sports agent, Leigh Steinberg. The agenda was pretty intense, and so was the content. Each speaker presented a unique perspective on the business of business. As I listened intently, taking copious notes from each presentation, I was struck by the realization that these were the Michael Jordans, the Tiger Woods, the Sir Anthony Hopkins of the business world – each crazy successful in his own right.

In speaking personally with some of them, I came to realize that they all had one thing in common – they thought differently.

That sounds like a business cliché, but in this case, it's true. The very language they used, the way they carried themselves and their very presence conveyed a sense of being 'unstoppable.' In fact, everyone in the room, many not speaking but successful entrepreneurs in their own right, carried an 'air of accomplishment.' I gained as much from conversations during short breaks and lunch as I did in session. The networking and free flow of idea sharing were impressive, more than I had ever seen at any other meeting.

On the flight home, I realized that this was more than just a powerful learning and networking experience. I realized that the best way to truly elevate my game was to exist in an environment of achievers – that there is a mindset, a way of thinking, a focus, an energy that high achievers have that is infectious. Infectious not of a 'rah-rah' nature, but owning a belief system that the impossible is possible. That the creation of something great requires big thought from the start, unencumbered by doubt. These high achievers believe that there is a way and that they will find it. They exude the traits of hunger, passion and unstoppable determination.

Most of all, high achievers take immediate action. They don't get bogged down in the 'planning process,' they take action; and that action, regardless of how small it appears at the time, leads to an outcome, which leads to another action, which leads to yet another outcome that leads to another action. With each action and outcome, progress begins to take place.

Moreover, progress catches momentum, and for some reason, momentum is attractive – people notice. Investors, clients, and the media soon become attracted to your idea and the progress that you have made. That leads to more momentum, more clients, and more interest. Think of Uber or AirBnB, or Ugg Boots – all were ideas, just simple ideas that have changed our lives and the way we live our lives, due to the action-outcome progressive formula.

This was my key take away while spending two days immersed in the midst of these proven achievers. Did they face setbacks? Oh hell, yes! Did they make mistakes? You bet – big ones. Listening to their respective stories, two common elements were obstacles and setbacks.

However, in every case, and I mean every case, it was mindset and the undying belief that there was a solution to each obstacle AND that they would find it. Not by planning and 'analysis paralysis,' but by taking action.

By no means am I suggesting that these entrepreneurs were careless gunslingers, casting fortune to the wind; far from that. Instead, they are calculated, determined, and strategic, but the big difference is action. This is the largest difference between the Mediocre Majority and these doers. The doers decide to take immediate action while the Mediocre Majority will make the decision to plan and plan and plan. The biggest difference here is that taking immediate action creates emotion, and it is emotion that drives results. Put emotion behind an idea and like water and sunshine to a seed, watch it grow!

My message is this. Love your family and friends with all your heart. Keep them close because they are the stability in your life. Be grateful for each and everyone one of them and the joy each has given you.

However, for your business, find new friends. Hang with high achievers who don't use words like 'try,' 'can't,' 'impossible,' or 'maybe.' Find a core group or what Napoleon Hill calls in *Think and Grow Rich,* a Mastermind group. (Hill 2009) Find new friends that care about you too, but won't stand for excuses. New friends that will hold you accountable for your actions. New friends that live with a belief system that you can create anything and have anything you want. New friends who won't buy your story of "I can't because . . ."

I don't know if it is serendipity, osmosis, divine intervention or some galactic force, but these associations will change you in a such a way that you will find the real you, the deep inside you that has been on vacation for most of your life. Release that real you and ignite your business. Ignite your life.

Don't get me wrong; you may already be achieving great things. In fact, I bet you are. However, there is another level for you, and the fastest way to get to that next level is to find new friends, new associations that through simple connection and observation will drive you forward.

EPILOGUE

In Brian De Palma's 1987 classic movie *The Untouchables*, a young treasury officer, Eliot Ness (played by Kevin Costner), frustrated at numerous failed attempts to bring in gangster Al Capone (Robert Di Niro), meets his mentor, James Malone, a streetwise veteran of the Chicago Police force (brilliantly played by Sean Connery), in the quiet sanctuary of a Catholic church. Here's their exchange.

Malone: You said you wanted to get Capone. Do you really wanna get him? You see, what I'm saying is, what are you prepared to do?

Ness: Anything within the law.

Malone: And *then* what are you prepared to do? If you open the can on these worms, you must be prepared to go all the way."

My question to you, dear reader, is, "What are YOU prepared to do to take your practice to the next level?"

And *then* what (else) are you prepared to do?

ABOUT THE AUTHOR

Robert Rullo is a nationally acclaimed keynote speaker, accomplished author and elite business performance coach.

With more than 30 years of business experience, Bob has brought his unique marketing style and strategic business insights, serving start-ups and Fortune 500 companies alike.

Focusing on healthcare, Bob founded The Aesthetic Blueprint™, extensively recognized as the *"most prestigious educational experience"* in aesthetics today. Working closely with hundreds of medical practitioners domestically and abroad, Bob is revolutionizing the business of aesthetic medicine.

Appearing in numerous medical and business conferences and journals, Bob Rullo uses his renowned imaginative thinking and infectious presentation style to teach aesthetic practitioners and business leaders, the strategies to creating geometric business growth while fully enjoying a truly enriched lifestyle.

For additional information & bonus content please visit:

AestheticBlueprintBook.com

REFERENCES

American Society of Plastic Surgeons. Plastic Surgery Statistics Report. 2016. Available at: https://www.plasticsurgery.org/documents/News/Statistics/2016/plastic-surgery-statistics-full-report-2016.pdf. Accessed 11/1/17.

Bova D. How do you build a loyal customer base from scratch? That's what the Las Vegas Raiders want to know. *Entrepreneur*; 2017; 29 June. Available at: https://www.entrepreneur.com/article/296567. Accessed 11/1/17.

Charon R. Narrative evidence based medicine. *Lancet* 2008;371:296-7.

Cialdini RB. *Influence: The Psychology of Persuasion. Revised Edition.* William Morrow and Company, Inc., New York; 2006.

Cialdini RB. *Influence: Science and Practice (5th Edition).* Pearson, New York; 2008.

Cialdini RB. *Pre-Suasion: A Revolutionary Way to Influence and Persuade.* Simon & Schuster, New York; 2016.

Comaford C. *Smart Tribes: How Teams Become Brilliant Together.* Penguin Publishing Group, London; 2013.

Dooley R. *Brainfluence: 100 Ways to Persuade and Convince Consumers with Neuromarketing.* John Wiley & Sons, Inc., New Jersey; 2011.

Dooley R. *The Persuasion Slide – A New Way to Market to Your Customer's Conscious Needs and Unconscious Mind.* Roger Dooley; 2016.

Dutton K. *Split-Second Persuasion.* Houghton Mifflin Harcourt Publishing Company, New York; 2010.

Dutton K. *The Wisdom of Psychopaths.* Scientific American/Farrar, Straus and Giroux, New York; 2012.

Dutton K, McNab A. *The Good Psychopath's Guide to Success.* Apostrophe Books Ltd; 2014.

Dweck CS. *Mindset: The New Psychology of Success.* Ballentine Books, New York; 2006.

Edelman website. *2017 Edelman Trust Barometer.* Available at: https://www.edelman.com/global-results/. Accessed 11/1/17.

Goldstein NJ, Martin SJ, Cialdini RB. *Yes! 50 Scientifically Proven Ways to be Persuasive.* Simon & Schuster, New York; 2008.

Haddaway NA. *Life (Everybody Needs Somebody to Love).* Song from the album Life. 1993. Lyrics available at: https://www.azlyrics.com/lyrics/haddaway/lifeeverybodyneedssomebodytolove.html. Accessed 11/1/17.

Hill N. *Think and Grow Rich.* Scorpio Moon Pub; 1937, 2009.

Kurkjian TJ, Kenkel JM, Sykes JM, Duffy SC. Impact of the current economy on facial aesthetic surgery. *Aesthet Surg J.* 2011;31:770-4.

Levin M. *Want to double your employee loyalty? Science says provide these 3 things.* Inc.com; Aug 2016. Available at: https://www.inc.com/marissa-levin/want-to-increase-employee-loyalty-by-67-100-science-says-to-provide-these-3-thi.html. Accessed 11/1/17.

Levin M. *9 Ways to Reinforce and Live Your Company's Core Values Every Day.* Inc.com; May 2017. Available at: https://www.inc.com/marissa-levin/9-ways-to-reinforce-and-live-your-companys-core-values-every-day.html. Accessed 11/1/17.

Livio M. *The Golden Ratio: The Story of Phi, the World's Most Astonishing Number.* Broadway Books, Danvers, MA; 2002.

Marquardt SR. Dr. Stephen R. Marquardt on the Golden Decagon and human facial beauty. Interview by Dr. Gottlieb. *J Clin Orthod.* 2002;36:339-47.

Newell-Legner R. *Secrets to Keeping Our Customers Happy!* 2008. Available at: http://www.rubyspeaks.com/csdvdhandouts/LeadersGuide-SecretsToKeepingOurCustomersHappy.pdf. Accessed 11/1/17.

Peters T, Waterman RH. *In Search of Excellence.* 1982, 2004:289.

Philips. Breathless Choir. Available at: https://www.usa.philips.com/a-w/innovationandyou/article/extended-story/breathless-choir.html?origin=1_us_en_bc_unr__btly_brc_es_sm. Accessed 11/1/17.

Pine BJ II, Gilmore JH. Welcome to the experience economy. *Harvard Bus Rev.* 1998. Available at: https://hbr.org/1998/07/welcome-to-the-experience-economy. Accessed 11/1/17.

Pink DH. *A Whole New Mind.* Riverhead Books, New York; 2006.

Pink DH. *To Sell is Human.* Penguin Publishing Group, New York; 2013.

Psychology Encyclopedia. *Pleasure Principle.* Available at: http://psychology.jrank.org/pages/497/Pleasure-Principle.html. Accessed 11/1/17.

Robbins A. *Creating Lasting Change: 7 Master Steps to Maximum Impact.* DVD Audio. Robbins Research International, Inc., San Diego; 2009.

Rovell D. Buyer pays #133K for two courtside tickets to Game 5 of NBA Finals. ESPN website; June 12, 2017. Available at: http://cdn.espn.go.com/nba/story/_/id/19616802/buyer-pays-133k-two-courtside-tickets-game-5-nba-finals-golden-state-warriors-cleveland-cavaliers. Accessed 11/1/17.

Runyon J. *How cold showers can change your life.* TEDx Talks; 2013. Available at: https://www.youtube.com/watch?v=Gb0h8ZKvJW4. Accessed 11/1/17.

Sinek S. *Start with Why: How Great Leaders Inspire Everyone to Take Action.* Portfolio, New York; 2009.

Swift A, Remington K. BeautiPHIcation: A Global Approach to Facial Beauty. *Clin Plastic Surg.* 2011;38:347-77.

Wickman G. *Traction: Get a Grip on Your Business.* BenBalla Books, Inc., Texas; 2011.

ADDITIONAL INFORMATION

Influence

https://hbr.org/2016/08/how-leaders-can-help-others-influence-them

http://www.influencehealth.com/insights/blog/jeremy-gordon/user-experience-is-consumer-experience

http://www.theelementsofpower.com/index.cfm/how-influence-works/

http://www.briansolis.com/2010/09/exploring-and-defining-influence-a-new-study/

For additional information & bonus content please visit:

AestheticBlueprintBook.com

Made in the USA
Monee, IL
30 March 2023